Who's Walking Who?

Victoria Hooper

ISBN: 979-8-7148-6564-0

Cover designed by Sam
www.fiverr.com/sam_designs1

Acknowledgements

This book is for all the dogs I've shared my life with…

Lady, Brandy, Jess, Pandora, Lunar, Cosmo, Celeste, and
Lily

Also, special thanks to everyone who has endlessly had to
listen to me talking about this book, including…

Perrin, Mum, Richard, Dad, Emma, Charlotte, Laura, and
Paul

Finally, thank you to Sally Smith and everyone else at
Canine Principles for the wonderful support and endless
good humour.

About the Author

Despite a lifelong love for animals, it has taken me nearly half a century to fulfil my dream of working with them. As a child, I trained every animal I could get close to, including our family dog, our rabbit, and our pet goat! Billy, the goat, certainly loved 'showjumping' in the back garden, but Twitcher, the rabbit wasn't quite so keen.

I had childhood dreams of becoming a vet, but formal education became difficult for me when I was sixteen, so I quit and found myself working in laboratories for a few years. I finally returned to full-time education aged twenty-five and gained a degree in Chemistry; I have never used my degree, but I had a great time at university!

In my thirties, I got married, became a mother, and got divorced. I qualified as an Early Years Teacher and worked in childcare and education while my child grew up, eventually becoming a childminder to enable me to work alongside my family commitments.

As my child reached adulthood, I finally decided in my late forties to follow my dreams and I re-trained as a dog professional. I am a qualified trainer and a member of the Institute of Modern Dog Trainers (IMDT). I set up Stargazer Dogs in the autumn of 2020, offering dog home boarding, daycare, and training.

Who's Walking Who?

I live in a small village on the south coast of Cornwall with my three dogs, Cosmo, Celeste, and Lily.

Contents

Introduction

It was Christmas Day morning down at the local beach and I was ambling through the dunes with one of my dogs – a typical morning for me. I was contemplating what an unusual year it had been for everyone (did I mention it was Christmas Day 2020?) and not taking too much notice of anything around me. It was early, and the beach was quiet, which is just how I like it. I noticed a man in the distance repeatedly shouting his dog's name, Fred. I began to take notice of the man and look out for his dog – my on-lead dog wasn't particularly keen on being ambushed by bouncy, off-lead, whirlwind-type dogs. I saw the man and then I saw his spaniel, trotting towards me, with a sense of purpose, but with none of the danger signs I associate with the all too well-known scenario of 'An issue for my dog'. It was brown and white, probably in his middle years, and he seemed like a perfectly likeable dog, intent on his own mission of exploring things that interested him and totally ignoring his human companion.

The man continued to call, over and over, and the dog continued to ignore him – it seemed like a well-rehearsed situation that had happened time and time again. And then it happened – the man, seemingly bored with his own constant yelling of the dog's name, yelled once again, "Fred, I'm not going to tell you again!" I couldn't help myself, I laughed out loud (the man was too far away to hear me, by the way, I'm not rude enough to laugh in his face!) I quietly said to myself "I bet you will" and sure enough, in less than 10 seconds, he called again, "Fred, Fred, come here". I continued through the dunes with a wry smile on my face. Even better, about a minute later, I saw the man reunited with his unrepentant spaniel – the man was bending down and wagging a finger in his dog's face, giving what appeared to be a verbal reprimand that I was too far away to hear and that I'm certain the dog didn't understand or care very much about!

And then it struck me - so many people have dogs and walk them daily with no idea how to get the best out of their walks. So many dogs, with well-meaning owners, are taken out regularly, but they don't get to enjoy their walks to the full. I'd been contemplating writing a book about dogs for a while, and now I had the focus I needed. I'll write about how to walk your dog – something that seems so very obvious but that so many people struggle with every day.

In this book, I will talk about every aspect of exercising your dog. I outline what equipment you'll need – is it better to use a collar or a harness? What sort of lead is best? Is it ok to take treats for my dog? Should my dog wear a coat or not? Should my dog wear a muzzle? It would surprise you how much having the right equipment, organised and ready to use, can enhance your walk. I also cover equipment that is best avoided, and I discuss why some commonly used items can be detrimental to both yourself and your dog.

I have an entire chapter talking about loose lead walking. I think this might be one of the most valuable skills to develop when you have a pet dog. If you can walk your dog easily, with the lead loose between you both, then you are far more likely to enjoy your walks. You will be happy to take your dog out and about often, leading to significant benefits for both you and your dog. In this chapter, I explain that good, on-lead walking doesn't happen overnight very often - it is a process which improves over time and we practice it over a lifetime.

I talk about your interactions with other people – how and when should you let your dog meet other people and their dogs. What should you do when someone else's behaviour impacts on your walk? I'll talk about where to go on your walks and how much choice you should give your dog when out and about. I also address how often and how far your dog needs to be walked each day and the type of walks that are most beneficial to you both.

There may be days when you cannot walk your dog, and the ideas in this book will help you meet their needs without leaving home. I describe why certain types of walks and activities are more beneficial to dogs. I talk about how to get your dog to walk nicely along with you, without sucking all the joy out of the experience for both of you!

Perhaps most important of all, I talk about how your daily walk should be the best part of your day. Even if you are super busy and struggling for time, then your walk will become the highlight of your day – the oasis in the storm of your daily chores. If you are one of those people who find that there are not enough hours in the day, then this book can help you use your dog walk for peaceful reflection and relaxation.

Just out of interest, this is not a training manual. Although I give suggestions about how to achieve certain things, it is not a "how to" book, but more a collection of observations about your daily constitutional and how it could be improved. If you'd like more information on how to train your dog, then I thoroughly recommend you look at "Easy Peasy Doggy Squeezy" by Steve Mann, or any of his other books. Likewise, I cannot speak highly enough of the information available at Canine Principles, founded by Sally Gutteridge, who has also written some excellent books about many aspects of dog guardianship. Sally's blogs are available at www.sallygutteridge.com and they are well worth a look!

It's funny how, when we get ourselves a dog, we have images of carefree walks in the countryside, with our faithful hounds romping along beside us, fit, healthy and attentive. What we don't pay as much attention to is just how much work can be involved in achieving this picture-perfect scenario. We forget that our dog is an individual, with his own needs, wants and preferences, and we will often need to tailor our walks to suit his requirements at that time in his life. If we get a puppy, it can take months, or even years, to reach this level of attentiveness and we may never achieve it perfectly. When we rescue an older dog, he will already have his own set of experiences and preferences shaping his behaviour and, whilst we can influence them to a great extent, our dog may never quite fit into our 'perfect' image of dog ownership.

This book should help people to improve their daily dog walks, by helping to understand their dog's behaviour, and their own, to achieve harmonious walks. I try to move away from the image of a dog and his 'master' and focus on the cooperation and collaboration that can be achieved between two species who have evolved alongside each other for many thousands of years. Having a pet dog should be an enjoyable, enriching experience rather than a stressful, tense conflict between beings who don't really understand each other well enough. It's time to let go of our previous misconceptions about dogs and leadership and relax into amicable dog guardianship.

By the way, I agonised over whether to refer to dogs in this book as "it", "they", "he" or "she". For the sake of consistency, I decided to refer to dogs as "he/him" but know that the advice given in this book applies to any gender.

I refer to my own dogs throughout this book to give examples and make observations about both dog and human behaviour. With that in mind, I'd better introduce you to the gang. I have the pleasure of sharing my home with three dogs. My beautiful, sweet, six-year-old Afghan Hound is called Lily. I have had her since she was five years old, when I rehomed her from her previous loving, but quite different home. She is quite unlike any other Afghan Hound I have encountered, being very affectionate and cuddly! She is also one of the most sensitive dogs that I have ever met. She loves to explore unknown places and meet new people, but they must be introduced slowly, with lots of time to simply watch and figure out every new thing she encounters. She is quite simply a sweetie!

I also have the absolute pleasure of residing with a pair of whippets - Cosmo and Celeste are siblings from the same litter and they are nearly two years old. I've had them since they were eight weeks old and they have always been quite different to each other. Celeste was the only girl in the litter and, since I wanted siblings of different genders, she was always going to be coming home with me. She is pretty, sweet, clever, and easy to train. She appears to be the most outgoing of my three, but I suspect it may be 'a front' and that in fact she might be the most sensitive of them all.

Her brother, Cosmo, is quite different. He is more aloof, and he takes longer to learn things. He was quite an odd pup (that's what happens when you let your teenager choose which puppy to have!) but he is shaping up to be a lovely, sensible adult dog. I hope he retains his 'goofiness' though, as he is such an entertaining boy!

On a quick side note, having two puppies at the same time is a LOT of hard work - it is easily more than twice the work of having a single puppy! It is not something that I recommend unless you have hours a day that you can devote to each individual's well-being. They need to be treated as individuals, and be socialised and trained separately to each other, to ensure that they do not grow up to totally depend on one another.

All three of my dogs come from a group of dogs known as sighthounds. These dogs are fast, skinny, and are rather lazy around the home. My previous dogs were also sighthounds - Lunar was a serious, sensible little whippet and her partner-in-crime was my first Afghan Hound, Pandora. Pandora was laid back and was a total 'princess' - she absolutely knew her own worth! She also happened to be the 'aunt' of Lily (Pandora's father was Lily's grandfather) but the two dogs could not have been more different from each other in personality.

Each of my dogs, past and present, have been quite different to each other, despite similarities in type, breed, and life experiences. It is worth reiterating that every dog is an individual. As you read this book, remember that your dog is also unique, and you will need to tailor your actions to suit you, your dog, and your own individual circumstances.

Ok, let's get ready to walk…

Chapter One

What You'll Need – Dog Stuff

Ok, so you're ready to have better walks. Let's have a look at the equipment that you'll need to have successful walks, day after day! There's more than you might think! If you get this part right, then your walks will always be much easier.

Let's start at the beginning and talk about a collar. I think many people are quite happy with this one and it is generally accepted that dogs should wear a collar most, if not all, of the time. Indeed, the law in the UK says that all dogs in a public place must wear a collar with the owner's name and address on it (there are exemptions for some working dogs). It might come as a surprise to some people that this law, which is part of the Control of Dogs Order 1992, is still in effect even now that micro-chipping your dog is also mandatory.

Not all collars are created equal! I strongly advise against any sort of collar which is designed to modify your dog's behaviour in any way. This includes choke collars, prong collars, and electric shock collars. No matter how big or small your dog is, teaching them to walk nicely on a lead is by far the best option, rather than using a collar which is designed to hurt or scare your dog into the 'correct' behaviour. A simple, comfortable, flat collar is great but make sure that it isn't too tight. Consider how comfortable it is – your dog will most likely be wearing it for much of the time, so this is especially important. It is widely suggested that you should be able to get two fingers between the dog's collar and his neck, but sometimes I think this may be a little too tight. On the other hand, if it is too loose, your dog may be in danger of getting it caught up on things such as trees, shrubs, hooks, and furniture. You know your dog best - there is a vast difference between a well-fitting collar on a big, fur-ball type compared to a smooth, skinny type! My dogs wear their collars quite loose for the simple reason that I never, ever attach a lead to them! Their collars are made from velvet and satin, and the sole purpose of each collar is to hold their identity tag! I only ever attach leads to my dogs' harnesses.

It's funny how so many people have a problem with using a harness on their dog. I can't think how many times that I've heard people say that using a harness makes a dog pull more. I'd like to say right now - harnesses DO NOT make a dog pull more. However, a dog who pulls wearing a harness will do less damage to themselves than a dog who pulls with the lead attached to his collar which puts pressure on the very delicate structures inside his neck. He needs all those things for basic life functions such as breathing and eating! I don't know about you, but I rather like my dog to be able to breathe and eat properly – I find it beneficial to his health!

There are some simple reasons why your dog may pull when you are out walking together. The first and main one is that dogs walk faster than people – it truly is that simple. The surrounding environment on their walks can be really stimulating to them, and it is very often the highlight of their day. Being able to use their nose to sniff around and find out about what's been going on since they were last in the area is one of their greatest joys. Imagine that you are on the way to somewhere that you really love – going on holiday, meeting a dear friend, off to get your favourite treat at the shop. I bet you walk faster than normal, right? So does your dog. The trick to not having a dog that pulls is to teach him that he will get where he wants to go quicker when he is walking on a nice, loose, relaxed lead. I'll tell you how to achieve this later in the book.

There are a tremendous variety of harnesses available, some of which are better than others. These days, we nearly all have the internet at our fingertips so do some research before you get a harness but keep an eye on what sort of websites you get your information from. I tend to look at posts from other people with the same or similar breed to mine and see what has worked for them as a starting point. I then check out the reviews for this product and see what pros and cons others have found. I'm always a little wary of who has written a review and their purpose behind it, but it's a helpful starting point.

As a general rule, I would say don't go too cheap when buying your dog's harness. The very low-end items are often poor quality, badly fitting, and may inhibit a dog's movement. Once my dogs are fully grown, I buy from the higher end of the price range, which seems eye-watering at first, but I know these harnesses are likely to last my dogs their entire lifetime and then it doesn't seem quite so bad.

I also like to look for harnesses with a Y-shape on their chest, which are fully adjustable to fit each dog extremely well, preferably with both a front ring and a top ring for lead attachment – I'll explain why in the next chapter. These harnesses allow for free movement in the dog, not hindering the shoulders in any way. I find that some of the harnesses with a wide band around the front of a dog's chest sit low on the moving part of the dog's shoulder. Anything which impedes the natural movement of a dog may cause health issues with prolonged use.

Finally, for my skinny little sighthounds, I like a harness with an extra band which fits just around the tummy, just behind the ribcage (not tightly). These are great for escape-artists like Celeste – she has a knack of slipping backwards out of more conventional, single-banded harnesses. I'm always so proud of her ingenuity when I see her do this - she pulls back away from the lead, stretches her front legs straight and fully in front of her and drops her head between her knees. A normal harness just pops off and she is free to go her own way. Much as I'm proud, I like to keep her safe and so I use a harness which really works for her.

Let's talk about leads. Personally, I like my leads to be at least two metres long and have multiple rings so that I can use them at different lengths. For a small dog, I might go even longer. These are widely available online – search for two metre training leads. I nearly always use these leads on their longest lengths, and this allows my dogs to make more choices when out and about. Also, it might seem strange, but when I switched onto longer leads, my dogs pulled less. It's likely that as they had more freedom to make choices, they were less stressed. Less stress can lead to a relaxed dog who takes the world in his stride, knowing he'll get to the good stuff soon and he's free to take his time getting there.

There are times when a shorter lead is appropriate, of course. Next to a busy road with multiple dogs? Then, of course, err on the side of safety and prevent your dog from ever being in danger of stepping into the traffic. Likewise, in the vet's waiting room, I tend to use a slightly shorter lead. This can be a double-edged sword, so use your own judgement for your dog on this one. If your dog is outgoing and happy to be at the vets, it's not ok to let him bounce up to other animals who may well be sick and/or stressed. A shorter lead may help stop your dog getting into bother with others, but you might increase his stress levels by limiting his choices in what is already a stressful environment. In the vet's waiting room, I focus fully on my dog and try to keep him near me with treats and reassurance, rather than a short lead. Your dog needs to know that you are there for them and will keep them safe whatever.

On to my pet hate – retractable leads, sometimes called flexi-leads. These things are the work of the devil, as far as I'm concerned. If you haven't come across one (and please don't go looking for one if you haven't), then these are the leads with several metres of thin, strong, string-like lead on a retractable coil inside a plastic handle. There is a button which allows the person holding it to stop the lead from rolling out, but in my experience, these are clunky and hard to operate in an emergency. I appreciate that people think they are great, allowing freedom for the dog without losing control, but the risks that these leads pose far outweighs any benefits from them! These leads give a false sense of security to the owner but, in fact, the chances are that your dog will already be in trouble before you find the button to stop them.

They roll out at great speed but then stop abruptly at the end, leaving your dog with a very nasty jerk to a halt when they run to the end. I've seen dogs get entangled with other dogs and other people on these leads, leaving nasty 'burns' where the thin cord drags against the skin of both dogs and people. I've even heard tales of dogs who died of strangulation when entangled in these leads, as it can be very difficult to release them once they are pulled tight around a limb or a neck.

To my shame, in years gone by, I used to use these leads. I regularly walked my two sighthounds together, each on an eight metre retractable lead attached to their collars as they didn't have good recall. One day, my little whippet, Lunar, took off after something while on this lead. Now a whippet has got the most incredible acceleration and a top speed of up to thirty five miles an hour. I have no doubt that she was running at top speed when she was jerked to a halt at the end of the lead eight metres later. She was less than two years old at the time, and the neck injury that resulted from this incident plagued her on and off for the rest of her life. Two or three times a year her injury would flare up. She would need sedatives and steroids to ensure that she rested and to treat the inflammation that occurred in the soft tissue in her neck. Working with my vet, we found that acupuncture and laser treatment helped, but my beautiful, sweet little whippet was never quite the same again. On top of this, repeated use of steroids has been indicated in the development of pancreatitis, the illness which took her far too young aged just eight years old.

Now I can't change what happened to Lunar – I was doing the best that I could with the information that I had at the time. I can, however, try to inform as many people as possible of the dangers of these leads, especially when attached to a collar, in order to try to prevent anyone else allowing such harm to their beloved dog.

So, what can you use if your dog doesn't have good enough recall to be allowed off-lead? I suggest you invest in a good long line and get used to walking your dog on that. I appreciate that the differences between a long line and a retractable lead may not seem obvious – they are both about the same length, after all. However, there are differences between them. A long line needs to be held with two hands much of the time, being loosely coiled to take up the slack and let out again as necessary. I sometimes let the entire length of the line drag along between me and my dog, but never near traffic or any other danger and with my attention entirely on my dog. When you are holding the long line, the chances are that you are focused on your dog – if you aren't then you are going to trip over it, I guarantee it! You are holding the coils in your hand so if your dog takes off, it is easy to tighten your grip on the coil of lead and not allow your dog into danger or to reach top speed. So many people using the retractable leads seem to be in a world of their own, chatting to someone or on their phone. Their dogs are free to dart any way they chose and often, by the time the person notices a problem, they are already up to no good.

Besides this, long lines are usually thicker and wider than retractable leads, so they are easier to handle and less likely to cause injuries to either people or dogs. Have you ever tried to stop a dog by grabbing the string on a retractable lead – I'll bet that you got a nasty injury to your hand if you weren't wearing gloves! My advice to you is give the retractable leads a swerve and invest in a good long line for the health and well-being of both you and your dog!

There are a couple of other things that you might want to consider getting for your dog for his daily walk. Firstly, don't be shamed into thinking that dogs don't need coats - this can be a popular theme on social media sometimes. It is, of course, quite true that dogs in centuries past didn't wear coats, but that doesn't mean that your pet dog now shouldn't be protected from the elements if needed. Our pet dogs have been selectively bred to have certain features and traits for quite some time now and a good, thick winter coat may not have been on the list of desirable features when your dog was developed for the show ring, as a working dog or as a companion. Don't get me wrong, if you have a sturdy, double-coated breed such as a Husky or Shepherd, then the chances are that he will cope just fine with an English winter. However, if you have a dog with thin, short fur, such as my little whippets or maybe a staffy-type, then please pop a coat on him if he looks cold or miserable. Truly, without their fleece coats, my whippets probably wouldn't leave the house for six months of the year! (I will admit that my pampered pooches are so resistant to going out in the rain that I've had a wooden shelter built just outside my back door so that they can pop out to toilet without getting wet, but I don't expect everybody to go that far!) So, please, get your dog a coat if it's appropriate for him and it will make his walks far more enjoyable.

The next item which people also struggle with sometimes is a muzzle. There is such a big stigma around having your dog muzzled and seemingly a lot of judgment attached to it. We need to see a muzzle as just another aid for dog walking, no different to a lead or a harness. Many people seem to think that it is cruel to muzzle a dog, but I think it's probably a lot more cruel to have a dog miss out on walks and exploration because we feel weird about using a muzzle. I see it as an insurance policy for some dogs – you pop it on your dog, just in case, but you don't expect it to ever be 'used'. I also insure my car, but it doesn't mean that I go out of my way to crash it just because I have insurance!

If you need or want to use a muzzle on your dog, there are some basic rules to follow. The best muzzles are the basket-type, which still allow your dog to pant, drink, and take treats. Beware of the fabric muzzles that keep a dog's mouth totally closed – these may be suitable for use for a short time at a vet's appointment, but they are not ok to use for daily walks. Your dog can only cool himself in very limited ways, including through his mouth by panting (and by sweating through the pads of his feet, but that's not really relevant here!) When out exercising, your dog needs to be able to breathe normally and drink as required.

When you first get a muzzle, please don't just force your dog's face into it and strap it on – this may cause your dog a lot of stress and fear, resulting in him not being keen the next time you try to take him out. Instead, take time to condition him to the muzzle gradually, using treats and praise. The idea is to get him to put his nose willingly into the muzzle every time by holding a treat at the bottom of the basket for him to take. You can practice this by dropping a treat into a paper cup and allowing him to 'dive in' to get it. I've also seen this done by smearing something yummy like pâté at the bottom of the muzzle as well. Then, with continued treats and praise, you gradually get him used to the straps being held closed, and finally buckled up. You can expect this to take a few days to a few weeks, depending on your dog, but it is absolutely worth the effort. When properly conditioned, he will look forward to having his muzzle on just as much as he likes the lead and harness! I've seen some great videos showing this process online – do your research and take it slowly.

One final thought about muzzles - the next time you see someone walking towards you with a muzzled dog, don't think to yourself "That dog must be nasty or aggressive". Instead, try thinking "What a responsible owner who is ensuring the safety of both their dog and others around them". Remember, there are lots of reasons a dog might be wearing a muzzle; some rescue organisations insist that their rescue dogs are muzzled in public, particularly ex-racing greyhounds, who after all, have been bred and encouraged to chase small furry creatures and they might not distinguish very well between a rabbit and your little fluffy canine! Other dogs may wear a muzzle to prevent them from consuming everything in sight, food or otherwise. So please stop the judgement and if you think your dog would benefit, don't hesitate to muzzle up!

Chapter 2

What You'll Need – People Stuff

Ok, so we've covered what your dog needs, now let's look at what you will need to make your dog walks easier and more comfortable.

The first must always be poo bags! I truly don't understand why there are still people who think that it's ok for their dog to poop in public and not pick it up. There is no reason on earth why other people should have to deal with your dog's poop. I used to be a childminder who took children out exploring every day, and on some days our walks were blighted by dog poop everywhere we went. Dog poop is extremely unpleasant and can be harmful to health, especially for children. There are no excuses for this – carry poo bags, pick it up and dispose of it properly.

While on the subject, let's try to be kind to our planet at the same time. I always buy biodegradable/compostable poo bags, which come in a cardboard box and have a cardboard tube in the centre of the roll. I make every attempt to reduce the amount of plastic that I consume, and this is one of the small ways in which I achieve this.

Also, please take plenty of bags with you – one poo bag is not enough! If I'm walking one dog, I take a minimum of four poo bags with me. You just never know how many you will need (and you may need to lend one to someone else sometimes!) Who am I trying to kid – most of the time, I have my four bags, plus spares in my coat pockets, in my trouser pockets, in the car and just about everywhere else I can!

Also, this may not be for everyone, but I have a "poo bag holder" which I take on every walk. Now this isn't a dispenser for unused bags, but a little bag made of wetsuit material, which I use to contain the 'full' bags after I've picked up. I have a genuine dislike for walking along, swinging a bag of poop as I go! Besides this, I like to have both hands available for managing my dog and his lead/long line. I know it's not a pleasant topic for conversation, and I apologise if you are eating as you read this, but dog poop is a reality of having a dog. It is your moral and legal responsibility to deal with it properly!

Moving on, another 'must-have' when I go out walking is a decent treat pouch – I take treats on every dog walk. There seem to be some people who think that this isn't necessary or that it spoils your dog somehow. The attitude is that the dog should behave well out of love for their human. I just don't get it! Why not use food treats to establish and maintain a great relationship with your dog? With a bulging treat pouch filled with high-value treats, I use my walks as training sessions and bonding sessions with my dog. The dog gets an amazing walk, filled with exciting sniffs, visual stimulation, exercise, and yummy food. It doesn't get better than this for a dog.

I hear people say that giving treats will make dogs fat. This doesn't need to be true. Eating too much and not having enough exercise can indeed make a dog fat. However, I am careful to make sure that I feed my dogs very small meals, usually less than half of their daily calorie requirements. The rest of their calories come in the form of treats, food puzzles, scatter feeding, etc. This ensures that I am meeting their behavioural and emotional needs, as well as their nutritional needs.

A small caveat to that – the treats that I feed my dog are usually homemade and they consist of tiny cubes of meat that I have cooked for them. I am very aware that since so many of their daily calories come from treats that they need to be of a good nutritional standard and not full of additives and preservatives. Be careful of the treats that you buy from the pet shop or supermarket: in order to establish a long shelf life, these treats are often full of additives and preservatives. Some chemicals used as preservatives are known to influence behaviour – it is similar in humans, particularly children. It seems a little ironic that we may use treats to help modify behaviour, when in fact, the chemicals in food treats may contribute to poor behaviour in the first place!

Another point that is worth noting, is that I feed lots of treats to all three of my dogs every day. Lily, in her middle years and having been spayed, is a little chubby and I'm reducing her calories gradually to correct this. Celeste is at a perfect weight and she looks a picture of health and well-being. Her brother, Cosmo, is skinny and bony! It's a struggle to keep weight on him, despite a great diet and copious quantities of treats. A dog's weight isn't just determined by how many treats that they get, but by a complex picture of overall health, genetics, diet, exercise, well-being, anxiety, etc. To deny them treats over a myth seems silly to me when it can lead to such great bonding and training opportunities.

Lastly, I carry great treats because if there is an emergency and I need them back to me in a hurry, I want to make sure that they return instantly, and I can 'pay' them well. If I don't, then the next time there is an emergency they may not be quite so quick to dash back to me!

Another advantage of always carrying a treat pouch is that it is also a safe place to put my keys, poo bags, etc. There are some great little dog walking bags and pouches on the market, which have pockets for treats, drinks, toys, phones and much more. I even have one where the shoulder strap has double-ended clips and it serves as a spare/emergency dog lead should you need one – genius!

Of course, another thing that you're unlikely to leave home without is your mobile phone. Now this may be a little controversial, but how about leaving it at home instead? I can hear you thinking, "But what if there is an emergency?" Yes, it's true that in an emergency your phone can literally be a lifeline. However, when was the last time that you had an actual emergency when out with your dog? How many dog walks have you done and not encountered an emergency situation? As I write this, I am approaching my fiftieth birthday and I got my first mobile phone when I was about thirty. So, I managed to go thirty years of my life without having the ability to make an instant phone call or being constantly available to receive calls from others. It's a very modern thing, this reliance on being connected at all times, and I'm not convinced that it's a good thing!

Now I know that you're highly unlikely to leave your phone at home, regardless of what I say, so how about a compromise? How about you take your phone, but you commit to leaving it in your pocket/bag and not using it at all during your walk? How about you focus on your dog walk and not be available for an hour or so – would that really be so bad? I'll be honest, this is what I do – I can't quite bring myself to go out without it!

But I have a strict phone policy on my walks – I don't answer it or check messages when I am walking and I focus on this little piece of the day, which is just me and my dog. Of course, there may be some people in your life who you need to stay in touch with, but I urge you to consider strongly whether a call or message can wait until you get home. For example, a message alert sounds, and you check the front screen without unlocking your phone. It says, "Mum, help, the kitchen tap has broken off in my hand and there's water pouring everywhere. What shall I do?" (This, of course, is a mockup –

no young person anywhere has ever used that much punctuation in a message!) Now, you'll be forgiven for grabbing your phone, calling back straight away, and telling your teenager where the stopcock is located.

Now consider the situation where your message alert sounds and you glance at your phone and see this "Hiya, fancy a catch up and a cuppa next week?" This message can wait without a doubt. Continue to enjoy your walk with your dog and answer your message when you get home. I've established a 'policy' where none of my friends or family ever expect me to answer a message straight away. Everyone knows I take a while and I'll get back to them when I've finished what I'm doing. There seems to be a lot of pressure to be always available, for all reasons, to everybody, and I think this is very stressful and probably detrimental to our mental health and overall well-being. (By the way, my family and friends also know that I often forget to get back to them later and if I haven't replied within 24 hours or so, they message again – oops!)

There are a few other things to consider which you might want to take with you. You may want to take a toy or ball to engage your dog on your walk – that's brilliant (avoid ball launchers though – please see the chapter on this later in the book!) Playing with your dog when on a walk is a great way to engage him and keep a good connection between you. If you are fun and engaged with him, then he is far less likely to wander off and make his own fun! There is a balance to be found here, though. It's not much fun for your dog if he has to spend the entire walk glued to your side looking up at your face. You need to find a way to strike the right balance between engagement and exploration – I'll give you some pointers throughout this book!

Another optional item might be a whistle, if your dog has been trained to recall to a whistle. If you do this, then I suggest that you use a little creativity when choosing your whistle. If there are twenty people in a park who all bought their whistle from the same large pet shop chain, your dog might get really confused if every whistle sounds the same! Try buying from a smaller, lesser-known source or maybe find a vintage whistle or even whittle your own! A little imagination on this one may pay dividends in the end.

If you are walking in the dark, there are a range of lights available to attach to your dog and yourself. This allows car drivers and others to see you – a must on those dark winter dog walks. On the same topic, some reflective items for you and your dog are a really good idea – my leads have reflective strips and I have a reflective bandana which I put on my black dog in the dark when out and about. Depending on how far you are going, you may need to carry water for both yourself and your dog – personally, I'm not keen on drinking out of the same bottle, but each to their own!

Finally, on the subject of what to take, make sure your own outfit is appropriate. You'll find that you're much more likely to want to take your dog out if you have weather-appropriate gear to wear. I'll admit I have clothes that I only use to walk the dogs – that way once I've finished walking for the day, I can go home and get changed, dry my hair and go back to my 'human' part of the day. Walking trousers/shorts are brilliant – they dry out easily and don't chaff when wet like a pair of jeans can. A decent coat will last for years, and it is well worth buying excellent quality if you can. I always wear walking boots or shoes, even in summer – I can't imagine how people manage to stay in control of their own feet and monitor their dogs wearing flip-flops? I'd be falling over every few minutes, for sure.

For summer walks, you may need sunscreen, but I must admit I question whether you should be out with your dogs in the hottest part of a summer day. Many dogs don't cope well and can quickly get heat exhaustion. In addition to this, the pavements and roads get very hot and can easily burn your dog's paws. The general rule is if it is too hot to hold your hand flat on the ground for five seconds, then don't walk your dog on it. On our very few hot days in an average English summer, please walk your dog early or late in the day, or not at all if the heat is extreme.

Don't forget a torch for those winter walks – not only can you see where you're going and see what your dog is up to, but it makes picking up poo much easier! A couple of years ago I came across a beanie hat with a built-in light – this has become one of my favourite bits of dog walking kit. It is brilliant for being able to see where you are going and keep your hands free to manage your dog. Of course, it also allows other people to see you - a must for safety in poor light conditions.

I know that this must seem like a lot of kit for just walking the dog, but it's all worth it, I promise. In my front porch, I have what I think of as my "tack room" (spot the girl who spent her younger years hanging around horses!) My dogs' leads, harnesses, treat pouches etc. are all kept together on hooks ready to use. Being organised and properly equipped means that your dog walks are more likely to be successful and enjoyable for both you and your dog.

Ok, now we're all ready – lets go...

Chapter 3

Loose Lead Walking

If there is one thing that will make dog walks more enjoyable for both you and your dog, then it is the ability of your dog to walk nicely on a lead. It seems so obvious, but it's one thing that everyone thinks should be easy, but it can be really difficult to achieve.

What do I mean by 'walking nicely'? Well, contrary to what some people appear to think, it doesn't mean that your dog must walk beside you, staying exactly 10cm from your left knee, looking up at you the whole time. This is a pretty miserable way for a dog to walk, with no chance to explore, sniff or otherwise experience the great outdoors. I guess the origin of this comes from obedience training, where dogs walk to heel as one of the objectives.

It's not that I have a problem with a dog being focused on the owner – sometimes it is really useful and can keep a dog out of a lot of trouble. My issue is with seeing people out with their dogs, yanking on the lead every second or two, saying "Heel" loudly and sternly and somehow thinking that this is an enjoyable experience for either themselves or their dog! For a start, simply yelling "Heel" at your dog every three seconds is a pointless exercise if you have not taught him to walk to heel when given this cue. I'm fairly sure that many people do this out of embarrassment that their dog is forging ahead of them, seemingly on his own mission (he is!) and they want to appear to be 'good owners' who are controlling their dogs. Secondly, there is no good reason for your dog to have to walk to heel all of the time when out and about – crossing the road maybe, but that's about it. But people, through no fault of their own, are using the information they have got, and unfortunately some of that seems to stem back to the 1970s and Barbara Woodhouse on TV!

In order to improve our walking experience with our dogs, we need to explore why dogs have such a strong tendency to pull when on a lead. The first, really obvious reason is simply that dogs walk faster than people. They have a natural tendency to trot along with purpose at a speed which is usually quicker than a human's walking speed. It really is that simple – it is not dominance, or your dog trying to be boss or trying to control their human. They just walk faster!

In addition to this, pulling on a lead is naturally reinforcing for a dog. I don't want to get all geeky and science-ey (I'm going to leave that for another book!) but there is a genuine reason based in science why so many dogs pull. The rules of Operant Conditioning define that any behaviour that gets a dog what it wants is reinforcing. By definition, a reinforcer will make a behaviour more likely to occur in the future. So, to put it simply, pulling on the lead got your dog where he really wanted to be nice and quickly yesterday, and therefore, he is going to do it again today to get where he wants to go really quickly. You can use this principle to help stop your dog from pulling if you know how! You simply make the quickest way to get somewhere happen faster when your dog doesn't pull. It sounds simple when I put it like that, and in principle it is. Applying this in practice, however, takes technique, practice, patience, and perseverance!

I think less talked about, but possibly just as frustrating, is a dog that lags behind constantly or refuses to walk altogether. This is probably slightly more complex than a dog who pulls. There might well be a number of reasons why a dog does this. He may be in pain and so reluctant to walk. He also may be unfit, in which case he would need to have his fitness levels improved gradually. A lot of dogs are very anxious about going out and about, and if your dog is reactive or fearful, then you need to address these issues so that your dog can enjoy his walks, not endure them. The situations talked about above can be serious, so get some professional help from a vet to check out whether your dog is in pain and/or a behaviourist to help assess your dog's anxiety if you think you need to.

Some dogs lag behind because they want to stop and sniff, and I can tell you categorically how I would cure that – I wouldn't! Let your dog sniff as much and for however long he wants to, even if you're waiting around for several minutes. Your dog has an extremely sensitive sense of smell and they glean a great deal of information about their world from their noses. Sniffing the ground is the doggy equivalent of reading the local newspaper – they can ascertain who's been here, how long ago, whether they are male/female and all sorts of other things. It is one of the most rewarding behaviours that a dog does, and we should allow them to do it as much as possible.

In both scenarios above, the thing we want to teach our dogs is to 'hang out' close to us and keep the lead between us slack. As I said above, it seems simple and it is, but it can be surprisingly difficult to achieve in practice. Remember when I said that it is extremely rewarding for your dog to pull – we need to make it even more rewarding not to pull. We'd like him to enjoy being close to us when walking on a lead and for him to make a choice to be nearby as we walk along. We do this by establishing a bond with our dog and making sure that he sees us as part of the experience, not just the chauffeur or facilitator.

Let's start at home by encouraging eye contact with your dog. In his book, Easy Peasy Puppy Squeezy, Steve Mann covers this really well and I suggest you check it out if you can. In short, have a plentiful supply of treats and get your dog's attention by giving him one or two 'for free'. Now hold some treats in your fist, slightly out to the side if you like, and don't give him any more for a moment. He'll probably be a bit perplexed – "Why has the buffet closed?" he might be thinking. He'll probably lick and 'mouth' your hand, trying to prompt you to release another treat but keep your fist closed. Eventually, he will glance up to your face to gather more information about what's going on. The instant he does this, say "Good" and give him a treat. Try to say "Good" at the exact moment that he looks at you, as if you were taking a photo of that moment in time – "Good" equals 'click'. This gives your dog valuable information about what he did that earned him the yummy treat. After a bit of practice, he will look at you every single time he wants to know more about what is going on.

This is such a powerful bit of training. We all think of a well-trained dog being able to sit, stay, lie down etc. but none of these actions have anything like the usefulness of eye contact. It is the basis of your entire relationship with your dog and the start of training every other behaviour. You want it to be his default behaviour whenever he is in doubt, so practice it for a few minutes several times a day. It also has the added benefit of improving your bond with your dog. On a regular basis, you provide him with yummy treats for nothing other than looking at you, and he'll want to do it more and hang out with you as much as he can. A solid bond of affection and trust will stand you in good stead for every part of your daily life with your dog, whether it is when you want a great recall or you want to reassure your dog when at the vets. Looking at each other gives both of you plenty of feel-good chemicals sloshing around in your brains. Now I'm not pretending to be an expert in neuro chemistry or such like, but I know that we definitely want more of the good brain stuff and less of the rubbish stress stuff in order to have a happy life – that goes for both you and your dog!

Once you've established regular eye contact from your dog, you need to dial it up a bit and try getting eye contact whilst you are both moving. Try this in the house or garden at first. Pop a lead, at least two metres long, onto your dog's harness, clipping it at the front of his chest, rather than on the top. This will become a signal to your dog that when the lead is clipped here, it must never become tight. Dogs are amazing at discriminating things like this – far more than we usually give them credit for. This is a really useful tip for training loose lead walking because it takes time to get results and there may be times when you just have to get your dog from A to B and don't have the time to practice your loose lead walking. So, give your dog a clear signal of what is expected from him – when the lead is clipped at the front, no pulling. If the lead is clipped at the top – great, go for it! If you use a method like this, then your dog will be clear about what you expect of him on any given day. As times goes on and loose lead walking becomes embedded in everyday life, you can probably fade this out if you want to. If you don't have a front ring on your dog's harness, consider if there is some other way of indicating to your dog what type of walk this is – maybe a different harness could be used for training walks or he could wear a bandana or similar when he needs to walk without pulling (I have nicked this idea from Steve Mann's 'Easy Peasy Doggy Diary' – thanks Steve!)

Ok, let's try moving now. With a treat pouch stuffed full of yummy treats, keep the hand holding the lead somewhere you won't be tempted to move it – maybe tuck a finger into your waistband? Now take a step away from your dog in any direction and wait for him to follow you. When he does, say "Good" and give him a treat. It is important that you consider where you hold the treat for him to take. If you hold it in front of you, then it's likely that your dog will hang out in front of you in anticipation of the next treat. It's probably better to give the treat beside you, somewhere between your hip and your knee, as this will indicate to him where you'd like him to be when walking. Repeat this over and over in a few brief sessions! As time goes on, you can move a few steps in any direction, including walking backwards, making sure that you are generous with the treats.

You are trying to improve your dog's focus on you and establish lots of eye contact. You want eye contact to become a reflex for him. Every time he wants more information about what is happening, he should look at you - "Why have we stopped?" - look at my human; "What's that scary thing over there?" - look at my human, etc. This isn't just about walking well, by the way, but a brilliant way of getting more focus on you. If your dog is in any doubt at all, he should look at you for more information, reassurance, and communication. It is a much better reaction than anything he may come up with himself when out and about, such as barking, lunging, or cowering. The idea is to establish such a great bond that your dog trusts you in every circumstance, no matter how unusual or scary. That way you can get him out of trouble and things like recall become much easier.

So now we have eye contact on the move, let's see if we can get all the movement in one direction – i.e. walking! Walk forwards and your dog will move alongside you (he should by now, you are the source of wonderful and tasty treats and you have been very generous so far!) If he doesn't, then you may have progressed a bit too soon – go back a stage and keep practicing. After a step, say "Good" and treat him. Keep walking and keep doing this, almost as fast as you can get the treats out of the pouch! Keep the treats coming as long as the lead stays slack. If the lead becomes tight, then stop and wait. Keep your hand holding the lead very still – resist the temptation to pull back on the lead to stop him. Eventually, if not immediately, your dog will glance at you as if to say, "What's up, why are we waiting?" The exact second your dog looks at you, say "Good" and hold a treat down beside you for him to come back and collect. Then, once he's beside you, go again.

When he's got the hang of it, try to reduce the treats slightly (this won't be on the first day of training probably as we are taking it slowly – we're changing habits for a lifetime of great walks, not running a sprint race!) A great way to do this is to use the 'three hundred pecks' technique. Walk forwards with your dog and if the lead stays slack for one step, say "Good" and treat. Then a further two steps, say "Good" and treat, then a further three steps, then a further four and so on. Do this until you can reach three hundred steps without the lead going tight between you. If at any time the lead goes tight, you go back to one! (If I ever happen to see you out and about, and I hear you talking under your breath, "One Good; one, two, Good; one, two, three, Good; one, two, three, four, Good" then I'll know what you're up to!) You'd be surprised at how effective this can be at getting great, loose lead walking and phasing out the treats a little!

There is a lot more than can be done to help with loose lead walking – if your dog is particularly inclined to pull then it can take a while and you may need to look up some other methods of practicing loose lead walking. The most important thing to remember is to be patient. My whippet boy, Cosmo, was a real puller. He's a skinny, bony boy, but you'd be surprised how strong he can be once he gets going. It took me months to get him to walk on a slack lead most of the time, and he still needs to be reminded occasionally. He just moves so quickly and is keen to get from one great sniff to the next. I realised that one thing that helps him not to pull, is for me to walk a little faster than my usual walking pace when out with him. Now I know some people may think that I should train him to walk at my pace, but I really don't see why. I base my relationship with my dogs on collaboration and cooperation, and that works both ways. His natural paces are such that my walking pace is somewhere between his walk and trot, and that's just not comfortable for him. By moving a little faster he is comfortable and relaxed and that's just the state I want my dogs to be in whenever possible. And for the record, walking a little faster certainly won't do my waistline any harm at all!

The key thing to remember is that this is a process and not a quick fix. Celeste, my little whippet girl, cracked this within minutes – she is sharp, quick to learn and eager to please me. She is also a master of eliciting treats from me whenever possible, and I love her for it! Her brother, as I said earlier, took months to learn. These are two dogs from the same litter, with an almost identical upbringing and range of experiences (no two dogs can ever have identical experiences) who are quite different to train. So, when you're out and about, watching what seems like everybody else's dogs behaving perfectly, remember that it is not always something you have got wrong but just that every dog is different. Love and work with the dog you have instead of wishing for a perfect dog – this doesn't exist except in fairy tales!

Chapter 4

The Best Part of the Day

It is a sad fact that most of us these days lead extremely busy, sometimes quite stressful lives. Many of us seem to work long hours and have many family and social commitments as well. It is strange but, in a world filled with labour-saving devices that my grandparents would have been astonished and possibly rather envious to see, we have less time to ourselves than ever before. We have automatic washing machines, microwave ovens and a freezer full of ready meals. The internet gives out information about virtually any topic in the world within seconds. There are cordless drills, saws, lawn mowers and vacuum cleaners, all designed to be used more quickly and conveniently. Our houses, gardens and garages are filled with things that are supposed to make life easier and yet we still don't seem to have enough hours in the day. It sometimes seems to me that in order to purchase these labour-saving devices, we need to work rather long hours, which, in turn, facilitates our need for labour-saving devices!

Now, don't get me wrong, I have absolutely no yearning to go back to the era of my grandmother, washing a family's clothes by hand, cooking and baking from scratch every single day, or sweeping instead of vacuuming (not that I do a lot of that either, especially now that I'm writing this book!) However, I think we could all do with taking a serious look at our lives and our priorities.

I am writing this at the very beginning of 2021, the year after the world as we know it changed because of the Coronavirus pandemic. I think last year will go down in history, just as the periods surrounding the world wars of the last century have, as a time of significant change for our population. It was a terrible, terrible year for so many people, who have lost people who they love, became less well because of longer lasting effects of Covid-19 and those who lost their incomes and livelihoods because of the need to isolate from virtually every other human, except those that they live with. It has been just awful for such a social species as human beings!

And yet, from all that is bleak during this pandemic, there are most definitely some tiny shoots of hope emerging. The enforced break that many people have had inflicted on them allowed time, possibly for the first time since their childhoods, to reevaluate their lives, decisions, and priorities. Their metaphorical foot has been taken off the gas and their bodies and minds have had the chance to rest and recuperate. What I see outside, as I look out from my own isolation, are people who have found comfort in nature and the outdoors.

Parents have previously struggled to get themselves and their children out of the door early in the morning to school, nursery and work. After a long day, they do their best to pull it all together and ensure that everyone is fed, bathed and in bed by a decent hour. It was all so stressful. These same parents are now walking slowly, happily, and freely along the lanes and countryside. They are chatting to their children, walking their dogs, and getting to know their neighbours for the first time.

My only other experience of this widespread sense of community has been on the occasional 'Snow Days' that we see here in the South West of England. We get so little snow that we are not in the least prepared for it. A few centimeters are all it takes for the world to grind to a halt, with schools shut and parents unable to get to work. And then something magical happens. Everyone goes outside together, and they just play. People walk and smile and play goofily with their children. The stresses and strains are left behind and are replaced with laughter and fun. As a childcare professional, I have long since thought that we should schedule in some metaphorical 'Snow Days' to our calendar each year – days where parents and children can reconnect without the pressure of work, homework and strict bedtimes and mealtimes.

Actually, 2020 was a bit like several months of 'Snow Days' and I watched people decompress in front of my eyes. Aside from the grief and stresses that the pandemic brought, it also bought a sense of what we have been missing within our oh-so-hectic lives. People are reevaluating and restructuring, often through necessity, but I truly hope that some of the realisations of 2020 will have a lasting impact on the population's health and well-being.

Now, I've written 700 words or so in this chapter, without mentioning dogs – and this is a dog book after all! So, what I really want to say is, those of us who own dogs have the perfect opportunity to make some of those changes a permanent part of our lives – a little bit of a 'Snow Day' built into every single day! I don't think it's any coincidence that during the pandemic, many people looked to get a dog if they didn't already have one. Now, whether or not this is a good idea is a topic for a whole other book (I might write it, just as soon as I finish this!) but I see the intent in so many people. They have a yearning to get out more, to reconnect with nature and living things and to remember what it feels like to not be governed by the clock every moment of their waking lives.

So, I'm going to say this - make your dog walk one of the best parts of your day, every day. Walking your dog should not be just another chore on your endless list, which has to be completed before you can finally fall into bed at night. Make it a highlight, an oasis of calm in a sometimes otherwise hectic schedule. Make it a time when you're not available on the phone and you can't reply to your emails. Make it a time to be mindful – to exist simply in the moment with your dog. Let your mind wander a little and escape from reality for just a little while (not too much – you still need to be connected to your dog, after all!) Daydream a little, perhaps? But be careful with this one. Don't let your daydreams becomes rumination

- don't dwell on negative thoughts and people who have wronged you. This will totally negate the good that your walk could bring you. If another driver annoys you on the way to your walk, just take a deep breath, and think for a moment how much stress that person must be feeling today to do that. Mentally wish them well and then move on with your day without giving it another thought. If another dog walker lets their dog come bouncing up to your dog with no consideration, try feeling some empathy for them. They haven't yet learned good dog etiquette. When and if they do, their lives will be much enhanced but for now mentally wish them better judgement and move on - both physically and metaphorically!

Likewise, don't spend your walks mentally having arguments with people, whether it's your boss, your partner, or your teenager. When you mentally rehearse conversations like this in your head, your body experiences some of the same physical responses as if you are actually having that argument. It gets a burst of stress chemicals which will do nothing for your well-being. It will also make a less than pleasant association with this person, for something that they haven't actually done! You never know, they may surprise you with a better outcome than you were expecting, and all that angst and concern was for nothing – it was only in your head!

I'm not saying that we can all walk along, with a secret reggae soundtrack in our heads playing "Don't Worry, Be Happy" at all times, but I am saying be mindful of what goes on in your head. How you talk to yourself really matters and getting in the habit of expecting and rehearsing better outcomes and relationships will have a positive impact in your life – it may take a bit of practice, however!

I know of a therapist who made the following recommendation to someone who was struggling with their mental health. She suggested that the instant they wake up in the morning, they throw on some clothes and shoes and go straight out for a walk. We all know that feeling when things aren't going too well, or we are grieving for something or someone that we have lost - the feeling you get a moment or two after you wake in the morning is the absolute worst. Getting straight up and out gets your body moving and allows your mind to focus on something other than that terrible feeling of descending dread. If you have a dog, then you have the perfect reason to get straight out with them and start each new day with hope and determination. Another, perhaps little appreciated aspect of your daily walk, is that those brief encounters with other people can sometimes totally change your day. A smile and a nod, or a comment about the weather (we are British, after all!) can make all the difference on a potentially bleak day. Some people who you pass on your dog walk will remain people to whom you simply nod and greet in passing, but others might be people you have something in common with. A nod becomes a 'hello' which leads to a passing comment. Soon you may stop for a moment to chat and you could find that you have something in common, usually dogs, and genuine friendship can develop over a period of time. Some of my best friendships have developed from casual conversations with other dog walkers. When you are still at school, friendships and socialisation are easy - you could even say that it is enforced, whether you want it or not. As adults, it can harder and harder to make a connection with other people. In a world of technology and social media, it's easy to just make do with online friends, but there is nothing quite like chatting to someone in person. During these months of isolation, the thing I miss most isn't going on holiday or going out for a drink, but it's having a friend over and sitting at my kitchen table having a cuppa and a catch up. Just like our dogs, we are social creatures and we do best when we have good, reinforcing social connections with others.

You may think that you simply don't have time to enjoy a walk with your dog – there just aren't enough hours in the day. And I say to you, you are the person who needs it the most! I remember the days when I was a working, single mother, trying to run a household, get my child to school and myself to work, and it often felt like I had done a full day's work by 9am. I'll repeat myself here – you need this the most! Try to get up a little earlier perhaps – just twenty minutes will make a difference. And if you only have ten minutes to walk your dog today, then so be it, but make it a great ten minutes! It is not about how far you go – you don't have to make it all the way around the block. Maybe you'll only manage to get a couple of hundred meters or so. But if your dog gets to sniff well and check his 'pee-mail' and you get a few moments to relax into mindfulness, then it will have been a successful and worthwhile walk. The rest of your day will be so much better for it. Now put this book down and get out there!

Chapter 5

Choosing a Route

A while ago, I was meandering around near the beach where various paths intersect, and I chatted briefly with a lady who was walking her dog in the other direction. She had stopped to let me pass, and I hadn't noticed her waiting as I mooched and daydreamed. When I looked up and saw her, I apologised and mentioned that I wasn't sure if I was going down that particular path as my dog was choosing our route today. She seemed truly shocked that I was letting my dog choose where to go on our walk. "That's not for me" she affirmed, "I'm in charge of which way we go". I smiled and let her pass, and I started thinking about just why we seem to think we must be in charge of every aspect of our dogs' lives.

It's such a common attitude that I'm sure many people have come across and perhaps think themselves. In the UK, and perhaps the wider Western world, we seem to think that we must always be in charge and that we must also, perhaps more importantly, be seen to be in charge. How many times have you heard the phrases, "You've got to show him who's boss" or "You must be the Alpha in the pack"?

I also noticed that in my fifteen years of education and childcare prior to my dog professional career, I was very struck by how much we seem to need to dominate and be "in control" of our children too. It's not an attitude that sits well with me – it makes me rather uncomfortable. I have never believed that I must dominate in order to guide and instruct. I remember vividly when doing teacher training years ago that someone said something to the effect of "It's not important what you teach children, but it is important that you teach them how to learn. That way they have the skills to learn about anything they choose to". This has really resonated with me ever since, and I have transferred the same code of practice to being around dogs. As for my thoughts on the education system – well, once I'd completed my teacher training, I never spent another day as a teacher in a school classroom and I later withdrew my child, Perrin, from school and home-educated them. Actually, I facilitated Perrin to home educate themselves, however, I think that may be the subject of another book!

Back to dogs and our need to be in control. It is a sad fact that a study of wolves in the 1940s still has a massive, and sadly wrong, impact on how we treat our dogs today. Dr Schenkel wanted to study wolves and so he captured some adult wolves, who were not related to each other, and forced them to live in close proximity to each other. Their resulting behaviour was the basis of the "Pack Theory" that we still hear so much about. In fact, Pack Theory has long since been disproven, yet the myth still pervades our culture and is widely used to justify dog training methods, often by high profile, 'celebrity' dog trainers!

The problem occurred because forcing these wolves to live this way, which was totally unlike their natural way of living, meant that their behaviour was aggressive and confrontational. This is a far cry from how a normal pack of wolves exist. Normally, a pack consists of a breeding pair of wolves and their offspring and their siblings. Only one pair of wolves breeds, with the rest of the pack all contributing to hunting, raising the cubs and everyday life. Sometimes younger wolves split off from the pack to form their own pack, becoming part of a breeding pair and having offspring of their own. Wolves live in harmonious family groups with very little conflict and a great deal of cooperation and respect. This is a far cry from the aggressive, hierarchical wolves forced to exist near each other in Schenkel's study.

There is another huge flaw in the 'Pack Theory' method of training dogs, which assumes that sometimes dogs are trying to be dominant and control you. Quite simply, your dog is not a wolf! There is little doubt that dogs and wolves evolved from a common ancestor, however, they have been evolving on different paths for tens of thousands of years and they are quite different creatures. In fact, your dog is no closer to being a wolf than you are to being an ape! (If you look sideways at this point to view the human you are sharing the sofa with, and are thinking "Well, I don't know..." then please take my point as it is intended and not too literally!)

Your family dog has evolved to live around humans for a long time now. They are masters of reading human body language and are an extremely successful species, because of their ability to meet the needs of humans and therefore be fed, sheltered, etc. by them. The dog in your house with you right now is not a wolf, a dingo, a coyote, or a fox, but it is actually 'Canis familiaris' – the domesticated dog.

I want to say it loud and clear, right here and right now – there is absolutely no justifiable reason why we should 'control' our dogs with forceful methods, show them 'who is boss', or make them submit to our will. This whole practice is, at best, confusing for our dogs and at its worst, it is simply abuse. Please, just don't do it.

I digressed a little from dog walking, but it's just so important that as many people as possible understand that what we have been taught, have believed and are still being widely shown on television and social media about dominant dogs and pack theory is just not true. Your dog is your comrade and companion; you most likely invited him into your home because you wanted a loving, faithful friend. So now allow him and encourage him to be just that – treat him with love and respect his rights as a sentient being, doing exactly what he has been bred to do.

So now that we know that we don't need to control our dog for our relationship with him to be happy and successful, then why not let him choose his own walk? There's a pretty good chance that a walk is one of the major highlights of his day, so why not allow him to get the most he possibly can from the experience?

This is the point where I must let you know something that you may not want to hear. Your dog's walk is for him, not you! If you want to reach ten thousand steps to meet your own personal goals, then your dog walk isn't the place to do it. You'll have to do that on your own time! If you want to improve your cardiovascular stamina, then don't do it on your dog walk (is this a thing? I'm not sure that it is, but I've heard this sort of stuff said. I have little knowledge about these things – I don't think that I have broken into a run since my last compulsory PE lesson in school, over 30 years ago!) Don't get me wrong, there are times when your dog would love to go running with you – off-lead, with excellent recall, away from traffic and free to stop and sniff as he pleases. This sounds amazing for both of you. However, if you want to run with your dog on-lead, tied to you, and forced to keep up with absolutely no chance to stop and sniff, then you must ask yourself if you are doing this in your dog's best interests.

Years ago, before I knew better, I used to envy those people who walk briskly around every day, with their dog meekly trotting alongside at human speed. They were getting their dog walk done for the day, swiftly and without chaos. At the time, my own two used to crisscross around me, crossing leads, causing chaos, and looking so very disorganised! Pandora, my Afghan Hound, could and would, happily spend fifteen minutes or more, pacing up and down the same five metre stretch of grass, looking for the perfect 'poo spot' (In all the years I had her, I never did figure out the criteria for that one – what on earth makes the perfect poo spot?) Meanwhile, Lunar, the whippet, could detect and recover any and all food items discarded in the vicinity. She would dive into long grass or hedges to snatch a variety of food (and other unmentionables) as quick as a flash! As I say, I often wished that my dogs would just walk properly, like everybody else's seemed to! As I look back now, I'm glad that they got so much out of their walks – who cares about how it looked? The knowledge that I now have about dogs has convinced me that the chaotic, disorganised walks were the way to go! My dogs got to sniff and explore and check their 'pee-mail' every day.

So back to my current dogs. I often walk my dogs individually – it is a great way to spend quality time with each dog, and back at home, the other dogs get accustomed to spending time away from each other (this is particularly important for my whippet siblings!). This means that I go on 2 or 3 separate walks every day, which takes up quite a bit of time, but I consider it such a valuable use of my time. I can meet each dog's needs individually, spend some time observing them, and really make that individual dog my priority for the duration of the walk. It also allows me to let that dog choose its own walk.

Now, of course, I live in the real world and my dog cannot totally and completely choose where he wants to go. For example, he cannot lead me into other people's private gardens, nor can he stop and sniff for ten minutes in the middle of a busy road. In addition to this, unfortunately, I have timescales and lots of boring 'things that adult humans have to do' most days. He simply cannot be wandering around for several hours, not least because the other dogs are home alone, and I don't leave them for long periods of time. In general, each day I have an approximate time that each dog can walk for, usually around forty to fifty minutes.

But it's amazing just how much leeway we can give our dogs within these limitations. Sometimes, I walk to the end of my drive and let him choose the direction we go in. At other times, I drive to my local beach or park and when we get out of the car, he is free to go in any direction he wishes. It's so good for a dog to be given choices sometimes. If you think about it, we control virtually every element of their lives – what/when/how often/ how much they eat, sleep, play, socialise and virtually everything else. It is so very empowering for a dog to have choice, and this is such an easy choice to deliver. Being free to make choices will give him confidence, and that confidence will spill over into other areas of his life. If your dog is fearful, worried, or reactive, having some choices will help to improve his optimism and therefore his overall behaviour. We all know how good it feels to make a decision for ourselves, which turns out to be successful and how it so often leads to further, excellent choices. If your dog is already quite confident, then it can't hurt to let him further improve his optimism in this way.

Sometimes, I make a sneaky tweak to a walk to make it work for me! Dogs are very tuned into our body language and they will predict which way we will go before we've given it too much thought, by simply observing our body language. If I am truly giving him a free choice of direction at a turning or fork in the path, I face my body equally between the two directions, usually at a forty-five-degree angle to the junction. This way he doesn't get any clues from me and can have a free choice. If I want to influence his direction, I simply face towards the direction I'd like to go in. It's surprising just how often this works for me, without having to use any other means of directing him to go a certain way. Using this method, I can ensure that a walk passes a postbox if I need to, or I can influence when it's time to start heading back in the general direction of the car or house. I don't take over completely, but I indicate my preference and he is often happy to cooperate in my chosen route.

There are other times when I take over completely, when I see that it's not in my dog's best interest to go a certain way. Perhaps I've spotted a car in the car park that I know belongs to the couple with the wildly out-of-control dog which bothers him? Or maybe I know that school run is about to start in my village and there is nothing remotely peaceful about a walk where three hundred stressed-out parents are trying to deliver their recalcitrant offspring to this local institution before commencing their own busy day at work.

When I dictate the general direction of a walk, my dog takes it in his stride and makes the best of it anyway. I'm also happy to take over part way through a walk if I think my dog needs it. For example, I took my little whippet, Celeste, to the beach the other day and then changed my mind almost before she had left the car. She saw a distant dog and seemed to become completely over the top with excitement instantly. This is something that she hasn't done for many months now, and we have been working on it quietly for a long time. On that day, something was different for her. It's not up to me to decide that she shouldn't feel this way, but to help her manage her emotions right there in that moment. I immediately decided that a walk on the beach would be far too arousing for her – it's a large beach and there can be upwards of twenty or thirty loose dogs there sometimes. I chose instead to walk her in the other direction - she wasn't particularly impressed with this decision, but I know it was the right one. We passed a couple more on-lead dogs at a reasonable distance and she bounced and pounced in their direction, just like she used to before we worked so hard on calm behaviour with her. I cut the walk short and took her home.

That may seem to be a bit over the top, but I've learnt how dogs can quickly become overwhelmed by a process called 'Trigger Stacking'. This happens when a dog is exposed to several small stressors, or stressful incidents, in a relatively short space of time. Each one of these stressors releases adrenaline into his body, which stimulates the production of cortisol, the stress chemical. The adrenalin dissipates relatively quickly, usually within an hour or so, but the cortisol takes much longer, and it can take up to three days to leave his system. If several stressful incidents occur, then the cortisol doesn't have enough time to leave the body before the next dose arrives and you have trigger stacking. When cortisol levels are high, one more tiny incident can trigger a complete overreaction in behaviour. It's why dogs sometimes bite, and humans get road rage – you could say it's the straw that broke the camel's back!

So, when Celeste flew over her coping threshold virtually before the walk began, I acted quickly, took a different direction, and cut the walk short (in hindsight, I perhaps shouldn't have walked her at all, who knows?) I know enough to recognise that a dog who is 'over the top' in this way cannot be coerced into different behaviour – her body was too swamped with chemicals to allow her to do it. I'm not entirely sure why she was so close to the edge of coping that day, but a little reflection recognised that it was just after Christmas and we were completely out of routine. She had had a minor incident with my other dog, Lily, a couple of days before, which also probably had an impact.

I didn't walk her at all the next day, but kept her at home in her safe place, just playing with her brother and doing some extra enrichment activities - I talk about this in more detail in a later chapter. The following day, we walked for ten minutes or so around our village at a quiet time of day and I have been building her back up to her normal routine for the last couple of weeks or so. Yesterday, we ventured back onto the dunes near the beach, but within a minute of setting foot on the sand, an off-lead dog bounced into her space and set her off again. It's too soon and we'll go back a stage or two and go slower. There is never any rush – we have a lifetime to get this right and we want to enjoy the journey as we go!

Chapter 6

I Can't Walk Today – Now What?

When you acquire your dog, there is sometimes a perceived 'moral contract' involved, which says that you will walk your dog at least once every day. It's feels as though it's 'a given' that your dog should be walked every day without fail, despite the weather and despite everything else that is going on in your life right now. Even if you, like me, have a large garden perfectly suited to letting your dog run around and exercise, he will benefit from the opportunity to explore different places and meet a variety of people, dogs, and other animals. So, what about those days when you just can't walk your dog?

There are some occasions when you simply can't walk your dog every day. There may be a medical reason and your vet may have told you not to walk your dog for his own good - many dogs need a few rest days following surgery or illness. If your dog is accustomed to walking every day, this can be quite a troublesome time for him as even though he is medically unable to walk, mentally he is likely to still want to be in his normal routine. Alternatively, you might be the one who is not feeling too well. I cannot think how many times I have dragged myself out of bed when feeling terrible, just so that my dogs don't miss out on their daily walks. On the odd occasion when I've truly been too sick to walk, I've often phoned family and/or friends to come over and walk my dogs for me because I am so worried that they will miss out on the highlight of their day.

Now, I'm not a fan of 'fair-weather dog walkers', however, there are some occasions when it's just not a great idea to walk your dog. I am not talking about a bit of rain here; I'm talking about extreme bad weather on those days when the wind and rain can be dangerous. I live in a rural area and many of my usual walks are surrounded by woodland and trees. Occasionally, in extreme winds, these trees are blown down and, on those days, I won't walk in the countryside. Likewise, sometimes it is not safe to take my dogs to the beach as usual; extreme tides and high winds are simply not safe for coastal walks. Also, as I live on a rather steep hill in a rural area that isn't gritted, occasionally ice means that I cannot leave my property safely. On these days, I try to leave my walks a little later when the ice has melted or sometimes, I abandon the idea altogether.

Your dog may have experienced a stressful or frightening situation. If that's the case, it may be much better not to walk him for a day or two. I discuss this more in a later chapter, but it is always worth giving your dog a chance to decompress after a scary experience. If you push him to walk when he is feeling anxious or apprehensive, then you may do him more harm than good. Your dog may be quite fearful of the world around him. The thought of taking him to a dog park or open space to run with many other dogs might fill you and him with horror. Some dogs are just not suited to this type of exercise and, whilst you can build his social skills, a free-for-all with multiple other unknown dogs may not be a great idea for him.

If this is the case, you might want to investigate hiring a private dog-walking space. These spaces are becoming much more popular and are popping up all over the country. There are even websites dedicated to advertising these private spaces. The idea is that you hire a private, secure space for just your own use for a period of time, usually an hour. Ideally, these fields are securely fenced and gated, and you get to allow your dog the freedom to run, knowing that he won't have to deal with unknown dogs. It is worth noting that not all of these spaces are of good quality, and you should check a private dog walking field thoroughly before you let your dog off the lead there. I have come across advertised fields which only have one-metre-high fencing with barbed wire on the top. One metre fencing might be fine if you have a small dog, but for leggy athletes like mine, it doesn't even come close to being secure. In addition to this, the fencing should be secure for all dog types. If you have a very small dog, it may be possible for him to slip through the gaps if the fencing isn't of a suitable quality.

I suggest you check out these fields well and read the reviews before you visit. Then just book an hour initially in case it's not quite the right space for you and your dog. If you like the field, there are often ways of booking multiple visits at a discount, which is slightly easier on the bank balance. In summary, if you haven't come across this idea before and you think it might be of benefit, have a look to see what's available in your local area - you may be surprised at how something this simple could change both yours and your dog's lives.

As I've already mentioned, I am writing this book at the very beginning of 2021. The year that has just passed has been unlike any other that I've known in my half a century on this planet. The regulations around coronavirus have meant that all of our lives have changed beyond our imagination. There were times last year when, because of self-isolation, I could not walk my dogs in order to comply with the law and to help keep everyone in the community safe.

Let me tell you about my dog-walking habits. I have three dogs who I cannot safely walk together, so I walk them individually. My young whippet siblings benefit from being walked individually rather than together. This allows me to meet each of my dogs' needs and our walks are often part walk, part mooch and part training session! Sometimes, I cannot devote three hours or more to dog walks in a day. Believe it or not, sometimes I have to do grown-up things like work, housework or meet other people. In order to accommodate this, I've established a routine where not every dog gets walked every day. Please don't throw up your hands in horror at this idea - I'm not neglecting my dogs! Each day, one of my dogs gets a long, interesting walk to the beach, woods, riverbank or similar. I usually drive this dog to somewhere of interest so that they get to explore an interesting place. Another one of my dogs will get a shorter walk on that day, usually around my local village, and it takes about half an hour. My dogs love walking around the local village - it's their space, they know it well and they get to check in with all the local dogs and read their pee-mail!

The third dog doesn't get walked on that day. I give this dog a chance to rest and decompress. I ensure this dog gets extra enrichment or training sessions on that day and, providing that they are not injured or unwell, they get free access to my sizeable garden. My dogs each get walked on two out of every three days, meaning they get four or five walks per week each. I know that this might sound a bit odd coming from a dog professional, but I honestly believe that my dogs benefit from these days off. All three of my dogs are sensitive sighthounds, and the world can be a little overstimulating for them at times. I believe they are healthier because I give them the chance to have days off from excessive excitement and stress.

There will be days when you know in advance that you will not have the time to give your dog a decent walk. This happens to everybody and we all have to get on as well as we can in our busy lives. Perhaps you have an early appointment, or you need to do something else that is out of your normal routine? If you know you won't be able to give your dog an adequate walk, then preparation is everything.

For example, if you know you won't be able to walk your dog one day this week, make sure that he gets a decent walk the day before if you possibly can. That way he might benefit from a chill-out day following an exciting adventure day. Also, when you know you cannot walk your dog adequately, make sure you have some suitable enrichment available to keep him occupied while you are busy. I like to stuff suitable food toys and freeze them, or I will make sure that I have a new bone or chew available on these days. The best thing you can do at these times is to set your dog up to succeed - make sure that he has ample opportunities to use your garden or outdoor space and give him lots of suitable puzzles to keep his mind occupied.

Have you ever noticed that sometimes, even if you haven't been physically active, you still feel very tired? I'm willing to bet that this happens when you're concentrating really hard on something, perhaps driving a long distance or studying for an exam? I don't know about you, but high levels of concentration seem to make me even more tired than physical activity. The same can be true for your dog. If you occupy his mind with enriching activities, there is less need for excessive exercise. Your dog has an amazing sense of smell and the world of scent is really important to him. We can use this to keep him happy and occupied when we cannot give him as much exercise as we would like.

It's very easy to set up simple games in your own home. The

simplest of all is probably to just scatter some of your dog's normal food onto the grass outside. This allows him to search for the food using his nose. Instead of simply being presented with his food in a bowl, some of it is scattered over a few square metres for him to find. Be careful not to make this too difficult if your dog is not used to it - to begin with, let him see you scattering it and then, as he gets used to the game, you can make it a bit more difficult by scattering it over a wider area or scattering it when he can't see you. You can teach your dog the idea of finding his own food using a simple cue - "find it". To do this, start with your dog paying attention and watching you then drop a treat in front of him and say, "find it". Repeat this many times so that he associates the words "find it" with snuffling around on the ground for a treat. Once he's got the hang of it, you can make this game more and more difficult, and eventually you'll be able to hide the treats when your dog isn't looking and use the "find it" cue to send him out to search.

As well as scentwork enrichment, you can also give your dog something to chew. Chewing is really important to our dogs; their ancestors would have spent a significant amount of time chewing after they had hunted down and killed a prey animal. The act of chewing releases good chemicals in your dog's brain, which helps to make him relaxed and happy. You may have noticed that when your dog was young, if you didn't give him a suitable chew, he would find his own! Your shoes, furniture, and anything else he could get his jaws around would have been vulnerable to his instinctive need to chew. Even adult dogs still love to chew every day.

Your dog might like to chew on a raw bone (never give a dog cooked bones as these can splinter badly and may injure him). Also, beware of giving bones that are too big for your dog - the weight-bearing leg bones of large animals, such as cows, are too hard for his jaws and teeth - try giving ribs, necks, or tails instead. I like to prepare stuffed toys for my dogs to chew sometimes. There are a multitude of different toys available on the market which are designed to stuff with food or treats, and they allow your dog to access the food slowly over a period of time by chewing. You can buy ready-made food to stuff these toys or you can use food such as cream cheese or pâté. Alternatively, you can prepare stuffing for these toys yourself - simply blend some meats and vegetables that are suitable for dogs and form a paste. This paste can be spooned into the toys and the toys frozen. Make sure you take the toys out of the freezer at least twenty minutes before you give them to the dog to help prevent freezer burn to his mouth and tongue.

There are many toys available for dogs where the dog must push lids or sliders to access a treat. I have a few of these toys for my dogs, but I must admit that I find them a little frail for my tough little dogs! They are easily chewed up and they don't last long in my house. Instead, I try to make my own enrichment toys with things readily available around the house. One simple idea is to take an old towel, scatter a few pieces of food along it, and loosely roll it up. Your dog will have to unroll the towel to get the treats. You'd be surprised at how many dogs find this difficult at first, so try to set the puzzle at your dog's level. It should be slightly challenging for him, but not so difficult that he gives up and doesn't bother. You know him best, so you know how difficult you'll need to make this. My beautiful Lily, the Afghan Hound, is truly terrible at these puzzles and I have to make them very easy for her. As time goes by, however, she's getting better and she prances around in excitement at the thought of getting to her puzzles every day. My little whippet hooligans are truly professionals at puzzles – they've been doing them from the age of eight weeks old and I make the puzzles a lot more complicated for them.

I tend to use a lot of packaging that I receive through the post. Cardboard boxes, thick envelopes, cardboard tubes and the brown paper that is used for protective packaging are favourites in my house. I often make a 'Cardboard Village' for my dogs to explore. I pop some treats into a range of cardboard boxes, often padded out with brown paper scrunched up, and then arrange the boxes around the room. My dogs will take up to half an hour or so to rummage through the 'Cardboard Village' finding all the treats. The best thing about this is that after a few days of being mauled by dogs, the cardboard is already shredded to go out for recycling! There are lots of great sources of enrichment ideas for dogs - I suggest you look at Sally Gutteridge's book, 'Enrichment Through Scentwork' for lots more ideas.

So, the next time you have one of those days where, for whatever reason, you cannot take your dog for a walk, don't be too hard on yourself. There are lots of other things you can do to enhance his life when you're unable to walk him. I think sometimes that we need permission from someone to not walk our dogs every day. We think it is a dereliction of our duty if we don't take our dog out every day. I'm telling you right now that it's okay, from time to time, to keep your dog at home when you think it's necessary. When you do this, you should do everything in your power to ensure that this is still a great day for your dog!

Chapter 7

Bad Walks Happen!

No matter who you are and how well-trained your dog is, sometimes bad walks happen! It is simply a fact that you must accept and try not to let it adversely affect your future walks. It can be so easy to have a rubbish time out with your dog and then you start to second guess yourself or perhaps even be reluctant to take your dog out again the next day. There are many reasons this may happen, and many of them probably aren't even your fault.

How often do you wake up just feeling 'out of sorts'? Perhaps you have a headache, or your neck is sore from sleeping in a weird position? Or maybe your tooth hurts or you're feeling apprehensive about something that is likely to happen sometime? There are many reasons why today may not be as great as it might be. Often you understand what the issue is with you, although sometimes you may not, and you simply accept that it is the way you feel right now. We even have a phrase to describe this – we say that we "got out of the wrong side of the bed this morning" to describe that 'not quite fully functioning and possibly bad tempered' state of mind which we sometimes find ourselves in. It's great when we can accept this, perhaps tell other people that it's how we feel right now and somehow get through your day hoping the feeling will pass.

The funny thing is, we are terrible at recognizing that this happens to other people too, and it also happens to our dogs as well! When you're out and about, and someone you know quite well apparently totally ignores you, it's possible that you will be really offended and ruminate over and over what you could have done to offend them. You might postulate all sorts of reasons in your head about what you might have done or what may have caused this change in behaviour in the other person. You may sometimes get rather cross and think up many things that you could say the next time you meet, or you tell other people all about this alleged snub.

What we rarely consider is that most of what we think about why the person has blanked us is likely to be completely wrong! The other person may have all sorts of reasons why they didn't acknowledge you on that day, and the chances are that they are probably not about you! Perhaps they are feeling unwell or anxious? Perhaps they have received some bad news? Perhaps they have simply forgotten their glasses and didn't see you. Until you have firm evidence to the contrary, I would suggest that you give the benefit of the doubt and assume that their 'ignorant' behaviour was simply an oversight and probably nothing to do with you. Funnily enough, when we do this, we often find that our own state of mind will be unaffected by the behaviour. We don't waste our own energy getting troubled by it and we maintain our own equilibrium and good humour.

You may be thinking, why is this relevant to walking my dog? Well, the thing that we rarely recognize is that our dogs have bad days too. I get headaches sometimes for no reason that I know of – who is to say that my dog doesn't get headaches? Does he get toothache or sore gums – it seems like he must sometimes, given the amount of chewing he does. Did he hurt or twist a paw or leg when playing yesterday – it could make it sore today. Or maybe he is just feeling a bit anxious. We so rarely recognise that things we have a rational explanation for may be things of great concern for our dogs.

Perhaps we dropped a saucepan on the tiled kitchen floor with a tremendous clatter – our dog may not have seen it happen, or if he did, think it was related to his behaviour, and now he's feeling nervous and apprehensive generally. After all, he may think that the horrendous noise was related to his exact behaviour at the time, or that a new monster has taken up residence - we just don't know. It seems likely that it may alter his behaviour somehow if it bothered him enough. Sometimes the wind blows in a different direction and pounds into the house from a different side, causing roaring and rattling in windows and doors that don't usually rattle. As humans, we have seen a weather forecast and know that the prevailing winds have shifted for a few hours; our dog simply knows that something different is happening. If he is a slightly anxious type, this could cause him to be out of sorts and his behaviour may change.

Perhaps you've bought a new coat for yourself especially for winter dogs walks? It's fantastic and has a huge hood to protect you from the elements. But your dog might well be thinking, "Why has my human added extra bits to themselves – are they still my human? Has something changed? They look different now when they call me. It's not the same as I'm used to. I'm not going to run back to them". Of course, your dog isn't really articulating those exact thoughts, but you get my point. For a dog who uses visual clues as a big source of information, even something as simple as a new coat can be disturbing.

Your dog sees the world differently to you and all sorts of things may have happened, or be happening, that are different for him. We don't necessarily have to understand exactly what it might be, although if we have an inkling it might help. We do, however, need to accept that our dog has good and bad days, just like us.

Another reason our dog walk might be a bit rubbish is embarrassment, either yours or somebody else's! We seem to care so very much about what other people think of us, which is funny really because there is a fairly good chance that other people aren't thinking about us at all! There is a primitive part of us, left over from our ancestors, which makes us believe it is beneficial to be part of a group. We instinctively try to act like others, look like others and be accepted by others because in days gone by, our survival depended on it. Our physical survival is probably less dependent on this now, but our social survival remains 'tribe' based. I'm asking you right now to let go of embarrassment and go out and enjoy your walk.

I used to care so very much about how I was seen by the world. As a childminder for nine years, it was almost more important how I was seen to be caring for the children than how I actually cared for them, which is sad when you think about it. Out and about, not only did I want the children to have great, educational, fun experiences, but I also needed to be seen to be delivering them. There was, in fact, a real basis for my concern – a single phone call to Ofsted from anyone at all, whether it was truth or fiction, could have resulted in the loss of my livelihood overnight. It's a great deal of pressure to live with, and eventually the strain of being a childcare provider led me to burn out and give up the job. It's a shame – I loved being around the children; they were cared for, kept safe, and they had a variety of enriching, educational experiences in my care, but the pretense and the paperwork eventually took its toll.

It's been a real personal battle of mine to give up caring what people think of me – I think I've pretty much cracked it now, although I am prone to an occasional relapse of crippling self-consciousness! Recently, I've started walking my dogs on a long line much of the time. Believe it or not, I didn't use one for a long time, despite knowing how beneficial it would be. My reason for not using one was that I didn't want people to think I was 'getting too big for my boots' and being too 'trainer-y'. What if I couldn't manage the line efficiently when walking? What if I tripped over it and people saw? What if people laughed at me if I got it wrong? I hope as you read this you can see how ridiculous this all sounds as I describe it. After all, I really am a 'dog trainer' – I've studied and learnt, been assessed, and gained certificates which certify that I am competent at understanding how dogs learn and what motivates them. More to the point, I am committed to the wellbeing and welfare of all my dogs and all the other dogs that I encounter.

I have a license to home-board dogs at my house, a process which included a great deal of preparation, paperwork, a Level three qualification, and an inspection from the local council. By anybody's definition, I am a dog professional. I am hard working and knowledgeable, and I need to remember that every time I have those nagging, squirmy, embarrassed thoughts about how people see me.

I'll ask you to take a leaf out of my book when you are out and about with your dogs. Please don't be embarrassed, even if your dog is behaving like a complete numpty! Your embarrassment will only make the situation worse. It will lead you to behave in ways that are not beneficial to yourself or your dog, just for the sake of the surrounding strangers. If your dog is reactive to other people or dogs, focus on your dog, not on the people who may or may not be watching you. Try not to predict what other people are thinking about you – they may be looking on with empathy, ready to help in any way that they can even if it's simply a matter of helping you to make space for your dog so that he can feel more secure again.

Walking a reactive dog can be one of the least pleasurable experiences of dog guardianship. I know – I've been there. My first Afghan Hound, Pandora, was very reactive to other dogs while out on walks. She didn't start off this way, though. As a puppy, she was relaxed, friendly and loved other dogs. During the first year of her life, she regularly ran off-lead, delighting in being faster than every other dog around (underneath all that fur, Afghans have the physique of greyhounds and are born sprinters!).

I think I remember the occasion when she first had a scary experience with another dog. I now know that it was likely that something called 'single event learning' happened which affected her for the rest of her life. An off-lead dog came bounding up to her when she was on her lead and she was unable to escape. The dog, whilst not attacking directly, was pouncing and diving at her and she twirled and span on the end of her lead, screaming and seemingly terrified. I know now that I perhaps could have handled the situation better. With hindsight, I could have been more vigilant and seen the incoming dog sooner, giving me time to make space or go in a different direction. I also could have called to the dog's owner, hoping that they could recall their dog. I was a long way from any roads, so I could even have considered dropping her lead to allow her to deal with the situation in her own way. Unfortunately, none of these things happened and from that moment on, Pandora was reactive towards other dogs when out on walks.

We spent the next eight years or so, the rest of her life, avoiding other dogs and managing her walks with great vigilance to avoid conflict. This was such a shame, as she was, in fact, a really loving, sociable dog who was simply afraid. People locally tutted and frowned at her, and I think she was known for being nasty. Being an Afghan Hound, she was also very recognisable and I think she became a little notorious!

I can only wish that I'd had more knowledge about how to help her years ago, but we can't turn back time and I won't waste any energy imagining what I could have done differently. What I can do is perhaps give you some inkling of how to help your reactive dog, or how to help people you may come across whose dogs appear to be reactive.

Firstly, you need to know that there are things you can do to help and you can help to make your dog feel comfortable enough not to react as much. It is a complicated situation that is different for everybody and not really the topic for this book, but here are a few pointers to get you started. Try to give your on-lead dog as many choices as you can – avoid narrow paths where you must walk straight towards other dogs or people. Also, try not to hold your dog on a very short lead when they seem apprehensive – give them as much lead as it is safe to do so. This can seem scary, but a dog who has some choices is likely to be less scared. Always be prepared to turn around and walk the other way if your dog appears to need to, even if it means changing your route altogether.

There are techniques called desensitisation and counter conditioning that can be extremely useful for helping frightened dogs. It may well be that getting professional help is the best way to approach this – look for positive reinforcement trainers/behaviourists in your area. I suggest you look on the IMDT (Institute of Modern Dog Trainers) website to find one. If you are struggling to find one, feel free to drop me an email and I'll try to help – my contact details are at the back of this book.

I also highly recommend a book by Sally Gutteridge – "Inspiring Resilience in Fearful and Reactive Dogs". This book is insightful, thoughtful, and it is really good at helping you to understand your own dog.

Above all, please know that just because your dog is fearful and reactive now, it doesn't mean that it will always be the case. With patience and understanding, you can make a big difference to how your dog feels and therefore how he reacts.

Finally, the next time you see a dog guardian who is struggling with a reactive or unruly dog, have some empathy. That person is doing the best that they can, on this day, with the dog they have and the information that they have available to them. We can all be a little too quick to judge and who knows, tomorrow it could be you who is having a bad day, and you'd want people to be kind to you!

Chapter 8

Other People Out and About

It's a funny thing, but sometimes whether your walk is a pleasant walk or an awful walk will be determined by the other people around you. These complete strangers can influence your day, probably more than the friends and family that you live with. It may be that you fill your walks with apprehension about bumping into one person or another; it could be that you go out of your way to avoid certain people, certain dogs, or certain times of day, every time you go out with your dog. As we've discussed earlier in this book, your dog walk should be the best part of your day and it's a shame to let it be so greatly affected by other people. So, let's have a talk about dog walking etiquette - how you should behave and how you can reasonably expect other people to behave when out and about walking our dogs.

One of my biggest irritations when out for a walk occurs when other people allow their dogs, which are normally off-lead, to come bouncing up to my dog when he is on a lead. I don't know how many times I've heard the phrase "It's okay, he's friendly" called from some great distance away across a beach or a field. I have no doubt that those people love their dogs dearly and know that they are friendly. I also know that they mean well and that they don't intend to cause any upset by allowing their dogs to behave in this way. Unfortunately, the people who allow their dogs into the personal space of other dogs are being terribly inconsiderate.

They have no idea about the status of another dog. They are allowing their much loved, usually friendly, canine companion into a space which may not be safe. A dog on a lead cannot exhibit normal dog behaviour and body language. This means that the on-lead dog may well be forced to behave in a way that he doesn't want to, which can manifest in a variety of ways. I think we have all come across those frightened, defensive, and reactive dogs who lunge, snarl and snap when another dog gets too close. What you need to realise is that this reactive dog is not doing anything wrong.

Usually when stressed, a dog will resort to one of three behaviours. These behaviours are often known as the three 'F's, which are fight, flight or freeze. In a perfect world, a dog would not be forced to choose between these three options, and he would be free to decide how to react to an incoming dog long before it reaches him. Since he is 'tethered' on a lead, he cannot freely use his own judgement on how he wants to greet the other dog. Some dogs will resort to a reactive display and appear to be aggressive and unfriendly. Others will try to flee, but unfortunately, they can only get as far away as a lead allows. Perhaps most sad of all is the dog that freezes - he feels he has no choice but to endure whatever happens to him. This is known as 'learned helplessness' and it is very sad to see.

Unfortunately, many people see this response and assume that he is a compliant and obedient dog whereas, in fact, he is terrified.

I cannot stress enough how important it is that you do not allow your off-lead dog to approach dogs that are on-lead. When this happens, the on-lead dog cannot exhibit normal canine greeting behaviours, and so misunderstandings often occur. If you are reading this book and you don't take away any other point from it, then please never again allow your dog to run over to any other dog that has no choice.

I often see people who are trying very hard not to allow this to happen and they call, and they call, but their dog doesn't come back to them. I'm going to let you into a secret - when you recall your dog the first time, they should run back to you straight away! Maybe, just maybe, they won't hear you if they are a long way away, if it's windy or something similar, but the chances are that if your dog does not return the first time you call it, then they will not come back with repeated calling. If your dog doesn't come back to you, first time, every time that you call them, then the honest truth is that your dog's recall is not good enough to be allowed off-lead. I know some people struggle with this concept - they think their dog deserves to run, play, and interact with every other dog on the beach or the park, but it's just not the case. I cannot stress enough how much your dog should be kept under control on a lead or long line until you have trained an extremely good recall. As I mentioned in the introduction, this is not a training book, so I'm not going to try to tell you how to teach this. However, we live in a world with information at our fingertips - there are a wide variety of resources available to learn skills such as recall. Look for advice which uses positive reinforcement techniques, and not aversives that your dog will find unpleasant, scary, or painful. The best way to have excellent recall is to have a bond of trust and a dog that wants to return to you because you are a great person to hang out with, not a scary one!

Let's talk for a moment about what many people see as good dog play. We tend to think that it's great when many dogs meet up together in an open space and play, fast and furious and wearing themselves out. Without doubt, this scenario is sometimes brilliant for some dogs. What we often fail to recognise is that not all dogs will want to play with all other dogs, all the time. If you think about it, when you are out and about, do you want to greet every stranger enthusiastically? There is a good chance that you make a judgement about people you meet from a distance. There may be something about their clothes, their walk, their demeanour that gives you a clue about whether you want to interact with this person or not.

We really need to recognise that this happens for our dogs too. When left to communicate properly, without the interference of their humans, dogs will make a series of decisions based on body language about whether they want to greet another dog. The body language used can be subtle and is often missed by us humans. Your dog may not be feeling up to playing today - he may be more interested in sniffing. He may have looked at the approaching dog and thought to himself, "Not today, thanks" and want to remove himself and not interact with the oncoming dog. Your dog may not be very sociable, and that's okay. Also, your dog may not have grown up around certain other breeds of dog and he may find their body language and communication different and confusing. That's okay too. What isn't okay is for humans to force our dogs to interact with each other - not every dog wants to be friends.

By the way, if you have one of those antisocial dogs who doesn't much care for the big, free-for-all scrum at the beach or at the park, maybe your dog would still like to be friends with one or two other dogs. Just because he isn't particularly sociable, it doesn't mean that he won't want a select friend or two, chosen by himself, of course!

So many of the dogs that I see lack social competence, which is often reinforced by well-meaning owners. Frantic, energetic play which keeps going at breakneck speed is not normal for dogs; it is often the behaviour of dogs with poor social skills and a lack of impulse control. Great play between dogs occurs when all dogs involved give consent through body language, and it involves frequent breaks. Socially competent dogs take breaks from play to allow situations to calm down and to ensure that play doesn't 'go over the top'. Most of us have seen children play when, at some point, someone goes too far. It's great fun for everybody until one person oversteps a boundary and then rough play can quickly develop into conflict. Our dogs behave similarly. If your dog has not had the chance to learn from an older, socially competent dog, then it is your responsibility as their guardian to teach them how to play properly. To do this, make sure that all dogs involved are willing participants and that they aren't tethered or confined and forced to play whether or not they want to. Also, make sure that playing dogs have regular breaks by calling your dog away from time to time. Give him some praise and a treat and then allow him to go back to playing. Breaks in play are critical if you don't want play to become conflict.

So, when I started this chapter, it was supposed to be about people, not the dogs, however, when we're out walking our dogs then it is a combination of both of our behaviour which makes the difference. I know very well how easy it is to get into conflict with the guardian of another dog. Unfortunately, if we have enough poor experiences when meeting other people and their dogs, then we might start to anticipate that others approaching us will be inconsiderate. It's a real shame when this happens because we can make it our reality and come to expect all other dog owners to lack consideration. In the past, I have been drawn into shouting matches with other dog owners and, to be totally honest, it has never ended well!

Firstly, it has never, ever improved the situation for my dog - in fact, I'd go as far as to say, that is always made the situation worse. When this happens, not only does my dog have to deal with the socially incompetent dog around him, but he also recognises my stress and discomfort which compounds the problem. Secondly, living in a small rural community, I am highly likely to bump into that person and their dog regularly. This could make for some really uncomfortable walks, where I peep around corners, or assess whose car is in a car park, just to make sure that I avoid a particular person.

This has never worked out to be a good thing for me. As the years have gone by, and I have become more aware of both dog behaviour and human behaviour, I realise that it is in no one's best interest to get into conflict with somebody else in this way. No matter how inconsiderate or rude I feel someone's behaviour is, I no longer argue with other dog guardians. It may feel as though you have no choice, but in fact you always have a choice. Instead, I strongly urge you to choose empathy instead of anger - the person who you feel is being deeply inconsiderate probably doesn't know any better. They may not be well versed in good dog etiquette, or they may lack social skills themselves. In both cases, anger will achieve nothing.

Instead, when a strange dog comes bouncing up to you, try to focus on your dog instead. Allow your dog as much free will and length of lead as it is safe to do so. This allows your dog to position himself and use canine body language to communicate with the incoming dog. If you hold your dog on a tight lead at this point, you are removing his opportunity to communicate well and there is more likely to be a miscommunication between the two dogs. A long lead also allows your dog the choice of moving away, and if he wants to do this, please go with him and allow him to make as much space as he wants between himself and the other dog. If the incoming dog has approached very directly with alert, forward-pricked ears, leaning forward slightly over its front legs and with a high tail carriage, I suggest you try to put yourself between this dog and your dog. Please don't take any risks here – there is a tremendous difference between a rude dog with poor social skills and an aggressive one! Rest assured that most dogs fall into the former category rather than the latter! When you do this, you are not taking an aggressive stance but simply attempting to break the focus of the intent dog. Hopefully, the dog's owner will be on its way shortly to retrieve their dog.

Always allow your dog space to move and, if your dog is quite small, don't be afraid to pick him up if you feel it is appropriate to do so. You may have heard that you should never do this, however your job as a dog guardian is to keep him safe. Please don't let him fend for himself when he's scared - you wouldn't allow a toddler to deal with a perceived threat in this way, so please don't expect your dog to. It is always okay to 'have your dog's back' and to do everything you can to keep him safe.

When the dog's human arrives at the situation, please do not enter into any conflict. I can't think of any situation where shouting would improve things for you, the dogs or the other dog guardian! If the other owner offers an apology, accept it and move on, both figuratively and physically. If not, and some don't, simply move away as well as you can without saying anything. There is something about us humans - we always seem to need to defend our behaviour, even when we know we are in the wrong! Getting into a shouting match helps nobody, particularly your dog. Simply move on with your day with optimism and have some empathy for the other person who is so lacking in communication and social skills. Your dog will thank you for it.

Finally, do you remember when I said that your dog walk should be the best part of your day? If you allow other people's behaviour to influence your mood, then I am convinced that this walk won't be the best part of your day. Deal with other people with maturity and empathy and show them another way to interact without conflict. You never know what ripples you might send out into the world.

Chapter 9

The Trouble with High Energy Exercise

For a long time, as a society, we have had a misapprehension about how to exercise our dogs well. There is no doubt that our dogs need daily activity and enrichment, but I think that sometimes we get this very wrong!

When we get a dog, there is an opinion that, in order to be a good dog guardian, we must give our dogs lots and lots of exercise. This is a particular belief for certain breeds of working dogs, such as spaniels, shepherds and malamutes. There is no doubt that breeds such as these were bred with great stamina to sustain high levels of activity. I'm certainly guilty of this myself in the past, thinking that some dog breeds need many miles and hours of exercise every day. There is certainly nothing wrong with giving your dog this level of exercise if it suits your lifestyle. If you live in a rural area and you like to go hiking or long distance running regularly, and your dog can join you, off lead, then great, go for it.

However, many of us don't have this type of lifestyle. We live in ordinary houses in ordinary areas with ordinary jobs and, to some extent, our dogs need to fit in with our lifestyles. The good news is that we don't have to give our dogs excessive levels of exercise to keep them healthy and happy. Of course, they must have exercise, but it is perfectly okay if this is at a moderate level. Your dog will benefit from opportunities to explore places outside of your home and garden, to romp around, to meet other dogs and people, and to explore the environment with his nose. That's brilliant, that's good dog guardianship. What your dog does not need is to be a super athlete with extreme fitness levels. I'm talking professional, long-distance runner type of fitness levels or Olympian athlete fitness levels. The vast majority of humans live their lives without achieving this top level of fitness, and so can our dogs.

I can almost hear some of you thinking "But my dog needs a lot of exercise to tire him out – he'd be a nightmare without it". I completely empathise with you when you feel you need to tire your dog out, but what we need to remember is that you can tire your dog mentally as well as physically. In fact, if you try to tire him physically on a regular basis, you will end up with a super-fit dog, who will need more and more exercise to get tired! High levels of exercise can also bring a risk of injury and put a strain on the body, which may lead to suffering in later years. You may well serve your dog better if you focus on a combination of physical and mental exercise. Remember when I said about how sometimes mental activity can make you just as tired as physical activity, such as when you are studying for an exam or driving a long distance? This is true for your dog as well. To achieve a happy, healthy dog it is better to aim for a moderate fitness level which is maintained by a combination of exercise and mental stimulation.

This brings me nicely on to my pet hate - ball launchers. If you don't know what I mean, these are long, thin, plastic, spoon-like items which enable you to throw a ball much further than you can when throwing normally. I completely understand why so many people use these every day on their dog walks. I bet their dog absolutely loves balls and loves to chase them, and there's nothing wrong with this in moderation. Unfortunately, some dogs almost seem to have an addiction to chasing balls. These dogs can't help it - we have bred them with these instincts in order to do work for us. Many of these dogs, however, are no longer working dogs but are, in fact, family pets instead. Chasing and retrieving a ball fulfils an instinctive need for some dogs. It also provides an outlet for somewhat lazy dog guardianship! For some people, taking their dog to an open space, repeatedly launching a ball for 20 minutes and then taking him home again is an ideal exercise. Alas, you probably aren't doing your dog any favours when you do this.

Let's look at why. Firstly, as I said above, you'll be creating a super athlete who needs more and more exercise as he gets fitter. Secondly, you may create a dog who has an obsession with chasing balls. There is no doubt that running after and retrieving a ball can be a fulfilling experience for a dog, however, you can have too much of a good thing! Thirdly, repeating an intense activity very frequently can lead to lots of strain on the body - dogs who obsessively chase balls will do damage to their muscles, tendons, and skeletons.

Lastly, let's look at the biochemical impact of repeatedly chasing a ball. I've touched on this in a previous chapter, but it is really important, so let's have a closer look at it. Now, I'm not a specialist in this area, however I think we've all heard of adrenaline and how it affects us. It has the same effect on our dogs. This chemical is released into their bodies when they feel stress, whether this is good stress or bad stress. It's an incredibly useful chemical for survival - it gives enhanced strength, speed and stamina which can help them get out of an emergency situation. However, production of adrenaline in the body leads to the production of cortisol - the stress chemical. When their bodies have adrenaline in them, it dissipates fairly quickly; usually in a little over an hour, it's gone from their systems. Cortisol, however, takes much longer to dissipate, sometimes up to three days. When you use a ball launcher as the only means to exercise a dog, he will get multiple doses of adrenaline - one for every time you launch the ball. This leads to high levels of cortisol production, which will stay his body for up to three days. When you do this day after day, the cortisol levels have no chance to come down and they remain high. This means that he will exist in a continued stressed state most of the time. When dogs (and other mammals, including us) are stressed, some systems in their bodies are shutdown in order to cope with the perceived danger. These systems include digestion and immunity. A dog that exists in a state of stress may well develop long term health problems because of their poor immune system.

It is also very difficult for a dog like this to wind down after an exercise session. So often we think that after a good run, a dog should be tired and will easily settle to sleep. In fact, the opposite is true - a dog that has exercised hard will find it harder to get to sleep because of the adrenaline flooding his system. If you think about it, I bet you can't get straight to sleep after a tiring day or a stressful incident - most of us need an hour or two to unwind after a busy or stressful time before we can settle. Our dogs are the same, and we should consider this when we provide them with exercise opportunities.

In an ideal world, your dog's daily exercise will be a combination of walking, running off-lead, sniffing and exploring. There is absolutely no problem with taking a ball on a walk with you and throwing it if your dog enjoys this. What I'm suggesting is that instead of the entire exercise session comprising chasing a ball, that perhaps you limit the ball-throwing to once every few minutes and intersperse it with other activities. There are many ways to meet your dog's exercise needs, and not every outing has to be high energy and exciting. Many dogs would benefit from sometimes having a calmer walk. I know this sounds contrary to many things that we have believed about walking our dogs for a long time. If you have a high-energy dog, you may feel compelled to make sure he gets a lot of exercise every day, and it's hard to break this habit. We have been conditioned to think this is the correct way of doing things, but there are other ways of providing good quality outings for you and your dog.

Let's consider some alternatives. Your dog, especially if he is a high-energy dog, might benefit from some calming experiences sometimes, instead of excessive physical exercise. Remember when I said that mental stimulation can be just as tiring as physical exercise - let's use this to occupy and entertain your dog without walking or running for miles and miles.

Have you ever thought about taking your dog and a pocket full of great treats and driving him somewhere new? When you get to this new and interesting place, it is perfectly fine to simply sit with him in or near your car and watch the world go by. Make sure that *you* watch the world go by as well - no scrolling social media or checking your emails! Simply sit with your dog and take in the world. Remember to give your dog plenty of treats during this people-watching session; this will help to create a good association with whatever you are looking at, particularly if this is an unfamiliar environment that your dog has never seen before. This is something that we recommend for puppies when they are beginning to explore the world, but it can be equally beneficial to your adult dog. Your dog will be able to see, hear, smell, touch and possibly taste, a totally new environment. It may be hard to believe right now, but half an hour doing something like this might be more beneficial for your dog than hours of high-energy exercise. I bet when you get home your dog will need a nice long nap to process all of this new information.

If you look online, Steve Mann, has coined an experience known as 'The Rucksack Walk'. You can find details of this on YouTube or in his books - I simply can't recommend this highly enough. It's brilliant for young dogs, dogs who lack socialisation, high energy dogs and dogs that may need a confidence boost. I cannot think of any dog who wouldn't benefit from this activity. I also think you might be surprised at how much you would benefit from a 'rucksack walk' as well!

On those days when you'd like a little more movement, remember to ensure that your walk contains a variety of exercise types. It's great to have your dog walking closely alongside you for a few paces. It helps their focus, and it's a great habit for them to be in should you need them to be paying attention to keep them safe. Having said that, there is no fun for you or your dog if they must spend their entire walk ten centimetres from your left knee. Allow him to roam around, either on a long lead, or off lead if he has great recall, and let him explore the environment with his nose. This is true enrichment for your dog. It's nice to find a balance between the time when your dog can explore freely and when he is paying attention to you. Sometimes I call my dog away when he is exploring, reward and praise him, and then let him go straight back to the interesting thing he was sniffing. This actually gives him a double reward; he learns that paying attention to me doesn't necessarily mean the end of a great activity. He gets a treat and then he gets to go straight back to what he was doing. If you do this now and then on every walk, your dog will know that paying attention to you does not mean the end of the fun. This is vital for great communication between you both. It is also something that is very handy when you genuinely need your dog to pay attention to you, to ensure that he doesn't get himself into trouble.

You will find that when you see each walk as an experience, rather than a chore or a necessity for tiring your dog, you will both get much more out of life. You will greet each day as a new experience - it will be a fresh experience as you will never get exactly the same dog walk twice! There will always be something new to see, someone different to chat to, and a new day to discover. Make sure that both you and your dog enjoy it to the full.

Chapter 10

The Lead is for Safety

Some time ago, when scrolling social media looking at my usual stream of dog content, I came across a phrase and I wasn't quite sure how I felt about it. The post said, "Your dog's lead is for safety, not for control". Initially, I rejected this idea and my thoughts immediately turned to how this could be true? I thought to myself, "How do I stop my dog from going in front of traffic? How would I stop him from bouncing on strangers? How on earth will I stop him from stealing that child's ice cream as we walk past?" These things all seemed impossible without the use of the lead to control my dog's behaviour. I've since learnt that actually it is possible to 'control' your dog under virtually any circumstances without using a lead.

Now don't get me wrong, many of my dog walks are carried out on-lead. I only allow my dogs off-lead when I consider it appropriate to do so. This means that the environment and the level of distractions around us are not so great that I do not truly believe that my 'recall' cue will work and work well. If I am in any doubt whether my dog's recall is sufficient in the current surroundings, then I do not allow him off the lead. Funnily enough, the circumstances for each of my three dogs are different - they have different levels of concentration, and different things that pique their interest. I believe that it is highly irresponsible to allow a dog off-lead unless it has excellent recall in that particular environment and so, as I've said earlier in this book, I frequently walk my dogs on a long line. It is quite a big change to consider that a perfect walk would mean that this long line does not become tight for the entire duration of a walk. It seems impossible, doesn't it? However, this is now what I strive for on every walk.

In my opinion, long gone are the days when it is deemed to be acceptable to use a lead to correct a dog's behaviour. Fifty years ago, in the 1970s, the first television dog trainer I can remember was a lady called Barbara Woodhouse. I'm sure that many of us remember her no-nonsense style and short, clipped commands. She advocated the use of a choke chain to walk all dogs; this is a chain collar which tightens around a dog's neck when the lead becomes tight. From my childhood I remember seeing her pulling sharply on a lead to make a dog walk close to her side. Like many others, I took this to be the correct way to walk a dog. Fortunately, I know better these days! Under no circumstances will I ever use a lead and collar to punish my dog or to correct his behaviour. It is simply no longer an acceptable method of 'communicating' with a dog. This type of communication is based on fear and pain, and this certainly isn't what I want for my beloved companions. Besides this, as I mentioned in the first chapter, a dog's neck is full of very sensitive structures that can so easily be damaged with rough handling. You invited your dog to live in your home as your friend and companion - I can see no justification for inflicting pain on your dog in the name of training.

So how can we achieve this utopia on our dog walks? How can we walk a dog without the lead ever going tight? The key to this outcome is in your bond, communication and focus on each other. You need to be fully 'present' on your walk, focusing on your dog and taking in everything around you.

This level of focus and bonding doesn't just appear as if by magic when you're out on your walk; it begins on the very first day you bring your dog or puppy into your home. It's not really very important 'what' you teach your dog, but it is important 'how' you teach your dog. Building a bond of good communication is the key to desirable behaviour in your dog. Every interaction you have with your dog should, as far as possible, be a positive one. I know this can be a really difficult thing to achieve, particularly when your dog has made a mess for the thousandth time or has destroyed something that is dear to you! It is vital that you take the time to learn about good canine communication. There are some excellent books on this topic and some great online resources. I suggest you check out Sally Gutteridge's 'Canine Principles' website or indeed her book "Canine Communication: The Language of a Species". Good communication means that as well as teaching your dog to understand how you would like him to behave, you can also look at his body language and try to understand how he feels and what he needs.

Do you remember when we talked about loose lead walking in an earlier chapter? The first thing we aimed to achieve was eye contact. This is the beginning of good communication - if your dog isn't looking at you, there's a really good chance that he isn't listening to you either! (the same thing applies to children, teenagers, and partners, by the way!) When your dog is looking at you, he is communicating with you. He is watching your body language for clues and trying to work out how to behave and what to do next. When we reward a dog for eye contact regularly, then great communication is possible. I can't urge you enough to make sure that your dog looks at you as a reflex – encourage it to be their default behaviour in any circumstances.

Of course, eye contact works both ways! There is no point in your dog regularly checking in with you if you are not paying attention to him. If you are 'present' with your dog and have a good understanding of canine body language, you will notice where his attention is and be able to guide him before he gets into trouble! With a little practice, you will be able to discern things like whether his tail carriage indicates that he is feeling neutral, excited, or anxious? You will notice his ears and his eyes, and be able to predict his mood, and possibly behaviour, based on his posture and demeanour. This takes some knowledge and some practice, but it is worthwhile to improve your mutual connection.

When eye contact is embedded in your dog's behaviour, and in your behaviour, then walking on a loose lead at all times becomes very possible. This does not mean, of course, that you must look at each other every second during a walk, but rather that you check in regularly and are each aware of the other's behaviour. Your lead or long line can trail in a loop between you both because you will use good communication to keep your dog where you want him to be.

I frequently walk my dog on a five-metre long line as this is the sort of proximity where I would like him to 'hang out'. I am happy for him to roam around, crisscrossing or changing sides and exploring within the bounds of this five-metre radius, providing that it is safe to do so. It's a habit that I have created for both of us. As he approaches the edge of this radius, I use my voice or body language to slow him or to bring him back within my preferred circle. This general habit pays dividends when my dog is off-lead, as it means that he is comfortable to explore but will always stay within reasonable proximity.

Contrary to popular belief, a happy dog doesn't always have to be on the other side of the park or beach, playing frenetically with twenty other off-lead dogs. In fact, for many dogs, this is not desirable at all. I want my dog's safe space to be close to me; in this space I will keep him safe and I will protect him from any and every perceived threat. Within this radius he can trot around, sniff and explore at his leisure. I am always willing to wait while he engages his senses to the full - it is part of my commitment to him. In return, I expect him to focus on me when asked and to return to me as required. It is my habit to ask him to return to me now and then, give him a treat and some praise and then allow him to go straight back to what he was doing. This enhances the trust between us, which is vital to good communication and safe exploration.

So, when you are out with your dog, think about how you could achieve this level of communication. The sort of walk where the lead never goes tight and where dog and human are in it together, simply exploring the day. You trust your dog to stay within your circle and your dog trusts you to allow him the freedom to enjoy his walk to the full.

There is no doubt at all that this takes practise - lots and lots of practise! It also needs you to be fully 'present' not scrolling on your phone or chatting to other people. You need to be aware of the environment around you and to see potential 'trouble' as soon as, or preferably before, your dog does. If you see something in the distance that may concern or over-excite him, then ask him to come to you. Reward and praise him for coming to you. Allow him to look at his trigger and then give some treats as needed to keep his attention while it goes on by. Be careful not to give treats before he sees the trigger as you are not trying to distract him in this instance. What you are aiming for is that when he sees a trigger, he comes straight back to you, knowing that rewards will be given. This is highly desirable behaviour. Now when your dog sees that child with an ice cream, instead of jumping to steal it from them, he will come straight back to you for the liver treats in your pocket!

Eventually, your dog will be so good at this that sometimes he will come back to you expectantly and you will have to try really hard to work out what he has seen that makes him think rewards are coming! Even if you can't figure out what it is, reward him anyway! In fact, reward him every time he pays you attention - with a smile, a kind word, or a treat. With this behaviour fully established, your dog will focus on you and not on the multitude of other things that you'd rather he didn't interact with. In time, you'll notice that the lead between you becomes tight less and less often. You and your dog are tuned into each other, and you can predict each other's reactions far more easily.

As the human in this partnership, it is up to you to make sure that your own reactions are always suitable. Stress, anger, and shouting will all upset your dog and make him less likely to focus on you in the future. Try to deal with life with something of a sense of humour. If your dog rolls in a muddy puddle, then think to yourself "Oh well, he's a dog, and that's what dogs do"; if your dog finds what he considers to be a yummy pile of fox poop and grinds his neck and shoulders into it with relish, then try to laugh about it - it's probably about time he had a bath, anyway. If you react with good humour and not anger, your dog is far more likely to pay attention to you in the future.

What I'm describing above assumes that your dog is not highly reactive to things around him, such as other people or dogs. If your dog is reactive or fearful, you will need to approach this a little differently, perhaps with the help of a professional behaviourist. They will help you assess your dog's needs and keep him 'under threshold' while using counterconditioning and desensitisation to help him cope. This process is highly individual and cannot be generalised in a book such as this. If in doubt, seek help – if you don't know where to start looking, then I highly recommend that you start your search by looking up both the 'Institute of Modern Dog Trainers' and 'Canine Principles'. Both organisations are run by ethical, experienced professionals who put the well-being of dogs uppermost in their ideology.

If you take this advice, you will notice that, as time goes by, you'll see that your lead gets slacker and slacker. You and your dog can mooch and roam to your heart's content, in almost any environment, knowing that communication and trust form the basis of your relationship. When you reach this stage, your lead will truly only be used for safety, and all other communication will be about mutual cooperation. It's truly a lovely way to be.

Conclusion

So that's it, that's about all I've got to say. Who would have thought that there could be so very much to talk about on the subject of taking our dogs for a walk? Like so many things in life, there seems to be an expectation that we all 'just know' how it should be done; after all, clipping on a lead and walking isn't actually that difficult. What can be difficult is ensuring that our walks are enjoyable for ourselves and our dogs, as well as respecting others around us. We are all individuals, and so are our dogs, and so we need to ensure that we take everything and everyone into consideration before we walk out of our front door. I have seen so many people struggling to achieve agreeable walks, whether it's because their dog is dragging them down the street, or because they don't know how to behave when their dog is 'playing up'. I hope that the thoughts and ideas in this book will help many more of you to have fulfilling, pleasurable outings with your dogs.

We've had a look at the equipment that you will need to walk comfortably and successfully. It may seem obvious, and even a little boring, but getting this bit right makes such a difference to our daily excursions. A good quality harness coupled with the right lead is the first step to enjoyable dog walks. Personally, I have three dogs and I think I own something like fifteen leads! Mostly, I use the same leads over and over, but sometimes it can be handy in certain circumstances to select a different lead for a different activity. Such is my aversion to retractable flexi-leads, I'm going to say it one more time - if you have one of these horrible things, please just put it in the bin today. Invest in a long line and take some time to practise how to use it. Your dog and your bank balance may well thank you for it in the long run.

Also remember that if your dog benefits from wearing a coat or a muzzle, then please do not hesitate to use one. There will always be somebody who wants to offer you unsolicited advice as to why you don't need these, but you are your dog's guardian and protector, and you are the one in the best position to know what they need. Always remember, if you get your dog a new coat, new muzzle, or anything else that is novel to them, introduce it gradually and allow them to get used to it over time with plenty of praise, treats and rewards. If your dog develops an aversion to anything you take on a walk with you, you are likely to ruin the best part of his day and consequently, the best part of yours!

We have also talked about what equipment us humans need to make our walks as pleasant as possible. I urge you to always take poo bags and dispose of them wisely. For the life of me, I can never understand the people that pick up their dog's poop and then fling the bag into a hedge or a bush - why would you do this? Assuming that these bags are not biodegradable, this item will now take considerably longer to break down than if you had simply left your dog's poop on the floor (not an acceptable option but better than decorating our countryside with plastic bags!). Please be responsible - I can imagine a time where, if people don't take more care when dealing with their dog's poop in public places, local authorities will ban dogs from some public spaces, such as beaches or parks. None of us dog guardians want this, so please, let's do our very best to enjoy our open spaces without infringing on the rights and needs of everybody else around us.

Always take treats - your dog will love you for it! If your dog is off-lead and you need him to come back quickly, you might be extremely glad that you're carrying some of his favourite goodies. Don't take any notice of the people who will inevitably tell you that they don't believe in giving treats on walks – you'll often find that these are the people whose dogs have terrible recall and no doggy social skills. Smile sweetly at them and move on. Pack your dog's favourite toy and a whistle, if you know it is helpful to you, and remember to leave your phone in your pocket - this is your time alone with your dog and it's special. In summary, the more organised you are with your dog's equipment and your equipment, the more likely it is that you will have safe and happy walks.

Once we'd talked about making sure we're properly equipped, it was time to look at loose lead walking. I'll repeat once more that this is a life skill and not a quick fix. There is no merit in using any device, collar, lead or harness that gives the appearance of achieving this quickly. These devices, and the trainers who recommend them, may well appear to achieve instant results, but the damage that you do to your bond with your dog is not worth a quick fix. I know this sounds a little extreme; people have been training dogs with choke chains, headcollars and other devices for decades now, and they are even recommended by the trainers that you see on the television. However, I ask you to stop and think about why you got your dog in the first place. I'm willing to bet that you wanted a friend and companion to spend time with and relax with. Take the time and patience to train 'loose lead walking' properly and, apart from an occasional reminder, your dog will have a skill for life.

We've talked about how your dog walk can be the best part of your day. It gives you the ability to take a small part of every day and take your foot off the gas, forget the pressures of your everyday life for a while, and simply enjoy being in the moment with your dog. Instead of being yet another chore, your dog walk can easily be the most rewarding, essential, and fulfilling part of your day.

In addition to this, we have talked about how and when we can let our dogs choose where they want to go. We looked at the optimism and confidence that it gives our dogs to have some choices sometimes. Within the bounds of this freedom, I've talked about the responsibility of taking over and not allowing quite as much choice if it's not in your dog's best interest on that day. You are the person who knows your dog best, and with practise and time to consider, I know you'll be able to make the best choices for your dog.

I've spent a chapter in this book talking about those days when you just can't walk your dog. As I said earlier, I used to find this concept very difficult and felt that my dogs were entitled to two walks a day, every day - now I know better. A good day for my dog is a day that meets his needs and my needs comfortably and without stress. If that means that on a particular day my dog walk is rather short, or even non-existent, then that's okay. I've given myself permission to not walk my dog every day, and I'd like to give you that same permission. Please don't use this as an excuse not to exercise your dog or to provide suitable enrichment, but to give you the right to use your common sense and instincts when needed.

I've addressed the issue that sometimes you're just going to have a bad day! Likewise, your dog can have bad days too. The problem with bad days is that sometimes it stops us from trying again the next day. Everybody has bad days, and everybody has embarrassing incidents sometimes. The best thing we can do is deal with them with as much good humour as we can muster and just write it off as 'one of those days'. Try not to let embarrassment dictate your behaviour and likewise, try to recognise when people around you are behaving a certain way because of their own embarrassment. We can be so quick to judge sometimes when, in fact, a healthy dollop of empathy is the kindest option. Bad days happen for us, for our dogs and for other people around us. Let's all get into the habit of 'chalking it up to experience' and creating a fresh start the next day. By all means, reflect on how we could make tomorrow better, but don't dwell on it to the detriment of future outings. We are all human, after all.

We've had a chat about dog etiquette and what you should and shouldn't do when walking your dog. One of my absolute pet hates is when an off-lead dog, with seemingly no recall, is allowed to come bouncing into the space of my dog when he is on a lead. Please don't let your dog do this. It is amazing for your dog to run free, off-lead, but you should only allow this in public spaces if your dog has excellent recall - by this I mean they come back the first time you call, every time. If you and your dog haven't learned to do this yet, that's okay. You can keep practising and, in the meantime, keep your dog on a long line so that you can prevent this from happening. If your dog has inadequate recall, but you want to let him run freely, then please consider using a private field available to hire by the hour. Your dog doesn't have the right to invade the space of anyone else, or any other dog, just because of your perceived need for his exercise. By allowing your dog to do this, you are not giving him the skills he needs to interact successfully with his own species. One day it might be your dog who is unwell or reactive or scared, and I'm sure that you would hope that the people around you have enough consideration and respect to give your dog the space he needs. I'm sorry for the firm lecture, but it would be wonderful if we could all walk our dogs safely and enjoyably, regardless of our individual needs and personalities. After all, we all just want to have an enjoyable time - let's work together on this.

We've had a look at the different types of exercise that you can provide for your dog and compared the benefits and pitfalls of various activities. I hope that I have helped you to understand that lots of high energy exercise is not necessarily the best way to exercise your dog. If you create a super-fit dog, you will have to give him more and more exercise to keep him happy. Besides this, some very repetitive forms of exercise can become an obsession for some dogs. This could lead to unwanted behaviours and to unnecessary physical stress and strain on your dog's body. The best way to exercise your dog is, like most things in life, to use moderation. A range of activities including moving, chasing, and sniffing every day might well meet your dog's needs better than one obsessive exercise type. It is also far less boring for you and it enables you to get fulfilment from your daily walk.

Finally, I've talked about how we regard your dog's lead on walks. For a long time, we considered it normal and beneficial to use a dog lead as a form of control and also to inflict punishment. I hope that by exploring this issue you too can practise the concept of using a lead simply for safety. It takes a bit of practise, but I am confident that we will all get there in the end.

So, I've reached the end of my first book. I have thoroughly enjoyed communicating my thoughts, ideas, and knowledge to you. I hope that by working together we can enrich the lives of both our dogs and their humans. At the start of this book, I asked the question, "Who's Walking Who?" I hope that I've made my case that the best walks are the ones that involve mutual cooperation and collaboration. At our best, we are walking together…

Connect with the Author

Have you enjoyed this book? Would you like to stay in touch with me and keep the conversation flowing? That's brilliant – I'd love to hear from you!

You can follow me on social media:

@stargazerdogs on Instagram and TikTok

You can visit my website:

www.stargazerdogs.co.uk

You can email me:

stargazerdogs@gmail.com

If you have enjoyed this book, then please leave me a review on Amazon. I read every single review and it's great to hear what you think of the book.